Love and Lifestyles

Love and Lifestyles
Building Relationships in a Changing Society

Mary Judd

Saint Mary's Press
Christian Brothers Publications
Winona, Minnesota

To Rick, to our children, and to our parents,
for the relationships which have been so important to my life.

Acknowledgments

With special thanks: to the many educators in Minneapolis and St. Paul who, very early in the project, outlined their textbook needs for a senior marriage and lifestyles course, especially Robert Collopy, Margaret Holcombe, and Paul Hemmelgarn; to Margaret Holcombe, Maura Bremer, and Annamay Scott for their suggestions and encouragement on the manuscript throughout the writing; to Patricia Samples for contributing two interviews; to Mary Perkins Ryan for her contribution to the content of chapter 6; to all those persons from various

Acknowledgments continue on page 191.

Nihil Obstat:	Msgr. Roy E. Literski, PhD, STL
	Censor Deputatus
	January 1, 1981
Imprimatur:	†Loras J. Watters, DD
	Bishop of Winona
	January 1, 1981

The nihil obstat and imprimatur are official declarations that a book or pamphlet is free of doctrinal error. No implication is contained therein that those who have granted the nihil obstat and imprimatur agree with the contents, opinions, or statements expressed.

Eighth Printing — 1985

Edited by Stephan M. Nagel

ISBN: 0-88489-132-1
Library of Congress Catalog Card Number: 80-54285

Contents

Relationships 1
and Our Need for Others

New Questions About Relationships

This is a course about relationships. You hear the word **relationships** a lot these days. It seems that many people are talking, reading, and writing about relationships and the different things the word seems to imply: roles, sexuality, marriage, love, lifestyles, sex, commitments, self-fulfillment.

Many people are interested in these subjects, in fact. Recently a bookstore manager wondered what topics took up the most shelf space in his store. So he measured the shelf space devoted to each one, and found that the subject of human growth and relationships "won" by twenty feet. Translated into human terms, that measure tells us that large numbers of people are asking questions about how they should live with other persons in their lives. Growing to maturity, for many people, means discovering new questions about themselves and their relationships.

Have you noticed this in your own life? As you have grown and changed in the past few years, have you noticed that your relationships have changed as well?

Think of the people who are important to you: your brothers or sisters, parents, friends, classmates, co-workers, teachers. Are some of these relationships much more important to you now than when you were younger? Are some less important to you now?

Relationships are a vital part of our lives at any age. As children we related to other people in loving ways. We had close friendships. Perhaps we had older brothers and sisters we admired. We loved our parents without question. We could be affectionate, open, generous, loyal to others. As children, it seemed easy and natural to love the important people in our lives. In turn, their love for us seemed easy, uncomplicated. We often took it for granted.

But in high school, relationships began to take on a new meaning. As we approached physical and mental maturity, it became important to put relationships on a more mature basis. With sexual maturity, it was even more important to relate to others in ways that made sense of being male or female. Growth and change meant discovering new questions about ourselves and our lives, such as:

What does it mean to be an adult? a man? a woman? How should men and women relate to each other? What is a good friendship? Where does sex belong in a relationship? Can someone remain single and still be a sexual person? Can someone be a sexual person and a Christian outside of marriage? When should I marry? Should I marry at all? What do I want out of life? What part do my relationships play in my life?

No course can answer all these questions. This one does not pretend to. It is, however, a course based on certain beliefs about ourselves and our lives:

1) We need other people in our lives in relationships that are close and lasting. This course attempts to discover what is involved in building and keeping friendships with others.

2) We can learn things about ourselves, about friendships, and about the world today, which help us find happiness in the relationships we form with others.

3) We can discover tools or skills for living which help us make our relationships stronger and more lasting.

But none of these statements makes sense unless we understand the part other persons play in our lives. And nowhere can we find more convincing answers than in our own lives and from persons in our past lives.

Living Without Others?

"What makes us happy?" Supposing you took this question to ten different persons and asked them what it means to be a happy person. How many answers do you think you would get?

Supposing you asked each one of them how concern for others fits into a happy life. You would probably find their answers even more diverse. Some would say those who are most concerned for others are the most happy. Yet others probably would say that the happiest people are those who know how to "take care of number one"—meaning themselves.

Supposing, however, you asked "What role have others played in forming your happiness, your personality?" You would probably find unanimous agreement from all ten persons that they would indeed be different persons today if they had grown up in different homes, with different parents, friends, and influences than what they had.

Most people readily agree that infants, young children, and teen-agers are dependent on other persons for many things in becoming happy and ultimately independent persons. When we are young, obviously we depend on others for food, shelter, security. What else? Just how much of ourselves do we really owe to other persons?

The story of a boy named Victor made many people wonder about this question.

It was late in the year of 1798 when three hunters walking in the woods of Caune, France, came upon a wild-looking child grubbing for roots.

The child, about twelve years of age, leaped instantly for a tree when he saw them and tried to climb to get away. But they moved quickly and captured him, put him in restraints, and brought him back to the village. They knew this was no ordinary child.

In returning they shouted for the villagers to see what they had captured. Those who came were astonished, for the child they exhibited looked disgusting and slovenly. Balancing like an animal, he moved convulsively, trying to bite and scratch anyone who hampered him.

Given the name Victor, the child came into the care of a teacher for the deaf named Jean Itard, who decided to work with him. Convinced that Victor had spent most of his childhood alone in the forest with only animal contact, Itard was intrigued by his unnatural qualities. He began to write an account of his work with the child. He called it *The Wild Boy of Aveyron.*

To the dismay of the villagers and the keen interest of Itard, Victor seemed less than human. Seemingly without faculties we consider essential human traits, he had no memory of any word or idea, no attention span unless for something he wanted, no judgment, no ability to imitate. He seemed unable to reason—not even to climb a chair to reach what he wanted.

Victor's behavior lacked order, changing from excessive laughter to deep sadness without apparent reason. His ideas seemed related only to physical desires. He lived a purely animal existence, wrote Itard.

He lacked emotions, showing no human signs of affection to those helping him but, instead, indifference.

In sensory functions Victor seemed less capable than the animals, wrote Itard. His eyes were without expression, showing no concentration. Victor could not distinguish between flat or raised surfaces, between music and noise, between perfume and bad smells. His voice was guttural and uniform, and his reactions seemed limited to fears of things hindering him.

Itard worked with Victor for years and saw progress in his development. This is another story in itself. But Victor never developed what we consider basic social, intellectual, and physical qualities within the broad range of human characteristics we call "normal."

Humanness as a Gift from Others

Some speculate Victor was brain damaged. But if so, could he have survived in the forest so many years? Other stories about the fifty or so "wild children" discovered since 1344 lend support to Victor's story, particularly the Rev. J.A.L. Singh's account of two children, Amala and Kamala. Discovered in 1921 at five and three years of age, they howled at night, slept during the day, crawled on all-fours, loved raw meat, and, upon their discovery, ferociously resisted all human contact.

Whatever you believe about "wild children" or about how many of our human qualities are inborn, not nurtured, it is clear that a lack of human nurturing deprived children like Victor, Amala, and Kamala of necessary aspects of human development and a whole dimension of spiritual development. By missing loving care and affection in early life, we fail to recognize affection, comfort, joy. Nor can we learn to feel trust in others or concern for their needs.

This experience of nurturing—or the lack of it—is so basic to our growth that it even affects the image we develop of God. **A New Catechism** describes religious growth in these terms:

> **It is in the family that the way to the Other begins, who comes to us in all others. God who created and gave growth to the child through his or her parents is also known first and foremost through the parents.**

Our spiritual growth—the ability to trust, to love, to feel concern for others—is rooted in the experiences of love and care given to us. Usually it is through nurturing experiences in our early family life that we first learn to trust and love ourselves, and to feel concern for others.

If we are to be able to love, someone must first have loved us in a nurturing way. Nurturing love is unselfish: it allows the person to become aware of his or her goodness and of the ways in which he or she is lovable and worthwhile.

We need others to become human. Yet we are not shaped by them like lumps of clay. We also choose, at each step of the way, how we will respond to the persons in our lives. Notice how brothers and sisters can grow up in the same family, yet each becomes a distinct individual.

Others **do** play an immense role in who we become. When we consider the fates of the "wild children," we see that a "normal" human and spiritual life is a gift we receive from other people. But once this basic gift is received, none of us is ever "finished" like a fired clay pot from a kiln. The process of becoming human never stops.

Today there is a special awareness of this process of growing, this movement toward becoming "ourselves." Many people see this growth, however, as being totally centered in our own personal fulfillment, something apart from our relationships. Yet from Victor's story it is easy to see that human growth is closely connected with other persons.

To find happiness in life, we need to understand our **connectedness** in the human family. The key fact about relationships is that **we become the persons we are meant to be, through and with one another, not in spite of the other persons in our lives.**

Happiness, then, is tied somehow to our life and growth with others. For example, in childhood we lived with others as "receivers" from family, friends, everyone who loved and nurtured us. But maturity brings a new stage to our lives. As adult persons we need to become "givers" as well as "receivers." Having received the gift of humanness from others, it becomes our turn to begin giving back, to share with others the gift of becoming human. For a mature person, daily life means to give as well as take.

As adults we still need others to help us. But the more complete our own growth has been, the better we are able (1) to meet our own needs and (2) to respond to the needs of others. Real fulfillment is rooted in this kind of maturity.

One psychologist, Abraham Maslow, described it this way: We each begin life with a need for love which is like a hole to be filled. This is our "love need," which is first filled by our parents and then by our friends. The more that love need is met, the more we are able to share ourselves with others. In that way, we are freed to become givers as well as receivers of love.

For Christians, the need for love is reflected in the central place love holds in the vision of Jesus. Love was so important to his life and teachings that his followers identify God with love. The gospel of John could not say it more strongly: "God is love." In history, God has been identified with many things besides love—justice, law, anger, mercy, fear, and various combinations. That love is the beginning and end of Christian faith can have a strong influence on the value we place on our relationships. More will be said about this later.

Living with a History

It is easy to generalize about maturity. But to talk about it in real life is another thing. How can we be sure we are mature?

One of the best ways is to try to look objectively at who we are and what we value. Yet taking an objective look at ourselves is very difficult. We can be helped in this by standing back and taking an honest look at our own "personal history."

Each one of us comes to relationships with an extensive "history," a unique past which wields a strong influence on what we expect in our close relationships. Yet we seldom realize how much our relationships are affected by our personal histories.

At no time is the influence of our personal history on our relationships more obvious than when we approach marriage. For example, supposing you loved someone very much and decided to marry. The two of you would talk endlessly, absorbed in planning a shared future.

You would have disagreements now and then, but you would try to be objective in settling them fairly and lovingly. And the more each of you understood your own past, the more honest and accepting you could be with one other. Any time we begin to understand how we came to be the persons we are, it is much easier to accept the differences, and to admire the goodness, in others.

How aware of your past are you? Try this mental exercise to look at the past:

Imagine that tomorrow morning you wake up with amnesia, the past blanked from your memory. What would you need to know about yourself in order to *know who* you are?

To find out, you would need to search back through time, retracing the stages of your life. Suppose there were a time machine to help you do this—to let you see the past relived. Mentally, take this time machine back through time. There are many questions and statements here to help you probe your past. Some questions you will want to skip; some will be more meaningful than others. Some questions might be embarrassing, but try to be honest about your answers.

Knowing your family as you do, remembering your early feelings about growing up, try to reconstruct some of the things you experienced in your long childhood as you think it must have been.

Go back to your entrance into the world as a helpless infant—needing food, warmth, loving touches that communicated that you were loved and accepted.

You began life receiving everything, but you possessed certain traits and potential and, increasingly, you were able to choose how to react to this new world.

Was the world a place of warm and loving human beings? What did you first learn about yourself through other persons?

Come forward a bit in time—mentally place yourself in the family as a young toddler of eighteen, twenty-four, then thirty-six months. Were you reasonably supported in exploring sights, sounds, ways to use your body and to show your feelings? Did you have others to play with, to enjoy? Did you have toys and materials with which to explore the world and to discover skills? Were you relaxed with those around you, secure, safe? Or were you fearful? Were you encouraged to be a unique person?

During your childhood years, could you express your feelings without fear? How did you learn to communicate with others?

I'M NOT WORRIED ABOUT THE FUTURE ... IT'S MY LACK OF A PAST THAT DEPRESSES ME !!

Could you ask questions that worried you, say what you thought? Or did you learn to endure anger or lack of interest?

What did you learn about your own creativity and resources? Could you use your hands, body, and voice to create things and to express yourself? Were your attempts fun or frustrating?

What did you learn about affection? Did your parents show affection to each other and to you? Was it warm, natural, open? Was it absent? or hidden?

What did you learn about touch, about embracing, about kissing? Was touching a natural way to express affection? Did you learn that your body was something good? Or was it something to be ashamed of?

As a grade school child, you found a definite place in your family, perhaps with brothers or sisters in a certain birth order. Or perhaps you were alone with your parents or parent. But you learned by now that acting in a certain way would get certain results. In what ways did you show that you were an individual in your family? What relationships were you reacting to or against?

By high school age, you had learned definite things from your parents about masculinity, femininity, male and female, mother and father. You knew if there were "man's work" and "woman's work" by watching your parents in the roles they lived out.

You also learned whether sexual roles could be lived with freedom and sensitivity to one another's needs, or if they were rigid, routine responses to life.

Most of all you learned how your family and friends felt about you, and what that told you about yourself. And, choosing each step of the way, you learned to respond to the world around you.

Now, by the end of the high school years, you have opinions and feelings about these things and about the future. You have an opinion about what it means to be married, and if marriage is permanent or not. You have certain ideas about parenthood—what it means in a marriage, how it is lived, whether it is primarily a joy or burden.

You have views as to whether marriage can be very happy or

not, and which things lead to this. You have ideas about how adults communicate in a close relationship and what commitment means. You might have views on the causes of divorce and how it affects people's lives.

You have some views about sex in a marriage—whether it is a unifier or divider, a source of joy or discord, whether touch is an end in itself or means something else. You have some idea as to what sex means in a relationship—whether it is associated with committed love or is merely a thrill: something passing, superficial.

By now you have come to expect a certain standard of living, have certain ideas about what a "good life" means. You have certain values, views about what is most important in life. You have certain views about the meaning of faith in your life and about what it means to live the Christian life.

You have certain patterns of friendship and communication with others, patterns based on what has "worked" for you.

And most importantly, you have learned "if you are enough." And you have chosen, more or less, whether or not you will be a "giving" person to others, sharing what you have received in this long past.

Now if the time machine were to bring you up to the present, you would know many things about yourself. You would be aware of the origins of your views and willing to hold fast to some and to compromise on others.

And to the extent that you realized others also have a personal history, you would be more understanding in conflict, more supportive in stress, less threatened in disagreement, more trusting in change.

And having seen the past, you would also know that you are not "finished," but still "becoming." You would know you still can change what you do not like about yourself. The past seems long, but a longer future lies ahead of you—waiting to be created.

The "time machine" is not an entirely imaginary thing. Life itself is a kind of time machine. We carry the past into each new day, a past we have made from all that others have given us. With it we each build our future. What kind of relationships will we choose? Can we build them to be close, loving, and lasting?

And what if our past has been full of hurt? What if it seems hard to get close to others, or to expect another person to care deeply about us? What kind of future can we look forward to?

Answers do not come easily to these questions. But it is important to remember that unless a person has experienced an early and total lack of affection—like the wild children—it seems that it is never too late to become loving, sharing persons. After years of studying human behavior, psychotherapist Carl Rogers believed strongly that persons, if given the opportunity, have an almost undeniable ability to grow toward healthy maturity. This is also the promise of our Christian faith: that each of us can learn to experience Jesus' healing love and in turn become more loving persons.

In the following chapters, we will discuss how our choices and our values either support or undermine our attempts to form strong, lasting, and loving relationships.

FOR REVIEW

1) What does the story of Victor suggest about human nature?

2) In what special way do our relationships change as we mature?

3) Define the term *love need*.

FOR REFLECTION

1) Imagine that you live alone on an island. Food is readily available from among the native vegetables and fruits, and the warm climate makes your clothing needs minimal and shelter almost unnecessary. Write a note—to be sent in a bottle—containing the following information: (a) your name, (b) a description of the island, (c) an explanation of how and when you arrived on the island, (d) a list of people you would like to see and their relationship to you, along with a statement explaining why you would like to see each of them.

2) Write an autobiographical sketch using the "time machine" questions in this chapter to jog your memory. Be sure to include your earliest childhood memory and the six most unforgettable characters in your life story.

Relationships 2
in a Changing World

A World of Rapid Change

The world is changing rapidly these days, and our changing world is the backdrop against which we as individuals meet, love, and live with other people. In your mind, how does rapid change affect relationships?

While change itself is a part of life, today there is such rapid change in the world that it has affected many of the social supports on which most people build their lives—church, family, marriage, government, schools. It also affects the way we communicate with each other and the way we view making commitments to others.

Margaret Mead, a distinguished anthropologist, has described the special changes in the world today as being unlike any the world has known before. Changes today are the compounding effects of many events which occurred between 1940 and 1960. They include the splitting and fusion of the atom, the development of nuclear weapons, the invention of the computer, the key breakthroughs in our knowledge of the living cell, the expanding world population, the deterioration of the environment through neglect and misuse, the "shrinking" of the world and the expansion of the consciousness of the human family through travel and TV, the growing problems in the distribution and use of world resources, and space travel.

Mead, who spent her life studying patterns of human growth and relationships in primitive cultures as well as in North America, believed

no generation ever witnessed such profound change as has the generation of older adults today. Consequently people twenty years old or younger face a totally different set of experiences than people who are older:

> **There are no elders who know what those who have been reared in the last twenty years know about the world into which they were born.**

The world today is now so changed, Mead believed, that it is unlike anything that other generations have had to face. There are so many new issues facing the world today that older generations should view the younger generation as they would pioneers: "immigrants into an unexplored and uninhabited land."

Rapid Change Affects Relationships

This rapid change affects our relationships. One major effect has been loneliness, which prevails in both groups, younger and older. Both groups, wrote Mead, are "inevitably very lonely, as we face each other knowing that they will never experience what we have experienced, and that we can never experience what they have experienced."

The changes she talked about deal with the whole spectrum of human living today, ranging from the physical environment of the world and its resources, to the psychological pressures under which we love, marry, have children, work, and seek satisfaction in our lives. They touch the most intimate aspects of our lives: How do we live in sexual and marital roles? How do we understand sexual morality, sexuality, marriage, parenting, family? What do we expect from relationships? from society? Where do we look for happiness in this society? How do we solve questions of peace and war? How do we relate to the environment, to our institutions, and to the rest of the human family?

Because change has cut across all of these areas in one generation, it has had the effect of changing what seemed to be the "natural," "normal" ways of loving others and of building relationships. What was the "natural" way to love, marry, and raise a family twenty years ago does not work so easily any more. Many of the traditional supports of society which helped our parents and grandparents live in love relationships have been swept away. There are not yet new ones to take their place.

Our communities, neighborhoods, apartment buildings, churches, families are still organized for yesterday. They provide little emotional or economic support to single persons, to single-parent families, to two-career married couples raising children, to young children lacking care, nutrition, health, or to elderly persons living alone.

The stress on relationships is showing. One out of three marriages ends in divorce. By calculating past and future divorces that individuals are apt to have, it has been projected that close to 40 percent of all marriages of young adults might end in divorce.

For children, if the projections hold up, 45 percent of all children born in 1977 will at one time or another live at least several months in a one-parent family—in marked contrast to 67 percent of children who lived with both parents in 1976.

When so many people are finding it hard to build lasting relationships, it is only logical to conclude that all of us feel some stress. How much of this stress is caused by social change, we do not know. Even couples happily married ask themselves: Could it happen to us? Is our marriage going to work? What should each of us be getting out of this relationship? Is it enough?

Every Relationship Changes

Today more than ever before, it is important to understand the factors affecting our relationships. For instance, we need to know that:

1) Change is a powerful force in our lives.

2) We do not need to fear change. Even profound changes need not destroy or threaten our closeness to someone if our relationships allow for change. The freedom that comes with social change—new choices we face in sexual roles and parental roles, in forming relationships and living with others in our families and communities—is also freedom to build stronger relationships if we are responsible, imaginative, and willing to take risks. Change, the backdrop of our lives today, can be a means of hope if we take responsibility for our relationships.

3) There are tools and skills for building stronger relationships—ways to understand ourselves and others, and ways to nurture relationships.

What does it mean to form relationships that allow for change? Part of the answer might be found by looking at successful, long-term relationships. A few years ago, Carl Rogers became interested in what it is that makes a marriage relationship work.

What is it, he wondered, that makes a good marriage? By talking to married couples, he thought he might find some common threads running through happy marriages. So he asked several couples he knew about their lives and marriages.

In one of the conversations, a man named Eric described his fifteen-year marriage this way: "Marriage . . . is a process." His life in marriage, he explained, had been one which had moved him and his wife together through time, through change, and through the unexpected.

Their past life could not be lived over, he said, because in sharing this life they had both become different people. Each had grown as a person, changing in many ways: in what each wanted from the other and could give to the other, and also in how each related to the other and to the world.

Yet through it all, Eric explained, something in their life had remained the same. They had kept a commitment to one another. Together, they had built a changing but lasting marriage.

After listening to Eric, his wife, and the other couples, Rogers concluded in his book **On Becoming Partners** that a good marriage is like a "flowing stream." It is not a fixed or finished state in life, but rather it is a process—as Eric put it—in which two people move through the

future together, supporting one another, each committed not only to building a shared life and to the other's happiness in that life, but also to supporting one another's growth.

Seeing Relationships as Processes

Rogers' perspective of the "flowing stream" is an especially good one for us today. He gives us a real key to what it means to form lasting relationships in a changing world. Life for all of us today means meeting and responding to a new, unknown future, and our relationships reflect this.

Picture in your mind a flowing river, moving forward to meet the unknown, in twists, turns, through changing scenes. Is that river always the same? Is it always different? Or is it both: staying essentially what it is, yet somehow always adapting in response to each new setting? It becomes rough when it meets rocks, muddy as it meets sand. Yet the river always moves ahead, growing, carving out its own course and affecting the face of the land through which it moves.

We each need a sense of "the river" in our own lives and relationships today. For our relationships to flourish, there must be ways of living with others which help us as individuals grow, support, and love one another as we face social changes. They also need to allow us to love others not only for who they are, but also for the persons they want to become. Relationships, in short, must deal successfully with two powerful influences: change in society and change within ourselves.

Most of us have different ideas, however, about what a good relationship involves. We usually think good relationships do not change. It is upsetting, often frightening, to discover conflict—another form of change—in our close friendships, marriages, or communities. Most of us fear such change in people we care about. It is threatening to us. Good relationships, we like to think, mean we are alike, and we remain the same. When we discover we have disagreements or new feelings about our love relationships, we tend to bury them, thinking somehow we are failures. Some of us break up the relationship immediately, concluding that it has failed.

Yet think back on the relationships you have had with parents, friends, someone you loved. Have they ever really stayed the same? Have you remained the same? Why should any relationship be static or unchanging? Both persons in any relationship—friendship, marriage, family—meet new situations, have new ideas, discover new needs and feelings. Honest relationships have to reflect changes, not stifle them. Good friends, instead of fearing change, share it and help each other grow.

Change and Choice

Carl Rogers' "river" image helps us live with change by helping us to accept it as a natural ingredient in our relationships. It also suggests there can be permanence along with change. A sense of permanence is a human need, much like love itself. In times of change, just what is it that gives us a sense of permanence?

Regardless of changes in our lives, three factors do not change for any of us:

1) Human needs, especially the need for love, never disappear.

2) The values we choose to live by bring stability to our lives. In the next chapter we will discuss how the values we choose affect our relationships.

3) Our power to make choices is never lost.

The human power to choose is something we are all keenly aware of because we face more decisions and options than any people before us in history. Sometimes it seems there are too many choices: how do **any** of us know what the best life for us might be? the best values? the best career? the best lifestyle? In fact, one of the biggest decisions is whether or not we want to deal with many of the decisions we face because we **can** decide to let others—associates, institutions, society—make a lot of our decisions for us.

Yet once we become used to making our own decisions, the power to choose becomes a tool for coping with almost any of the circumstances we face. As an example, let's look at an especially harsh situation in human history. The anthropologist Loren Eiseley found evidence in a prehistoric site which gives eloquent testimony to the power of human choice:

Forty thousand years ago in the bleak uplands of southwestern Asia . . . a man whose face might cause you some slight uneasiness if he sat beside you—a man of this sort existed with a fearful body handicap in the ice-age world. He had lost an arm. But still he lived and was cared for. Somebody, some group of human beings, in a hard, violent, and stony world, loved this maimed creature enough to cherish him.

Someone chose to love and to be compassionate regardless of the cruel circumstances of pre-historic life. Today, like Eric and his wife, we also can choose to make commitments a part of our changing lives.

In the next chapter, we will discuss how our relationships reflect our values. And we will consider how the values society often places on relationships can contradict the understanding Christians have of the value of relationships and love.

FOR REVIEW

1) In what way are the younger people in our society "immigrants into an unexplored and uninhabited land"?

2) In what ways are relationships like flowing streams, according to Carl Rogers?

3) What three human factors never change?

FOR REFLECTION

1) Write a biographical sketch of one of your parents describing him or her at your age. What size city or town did your parent live in? How did your parent spend a typical evening or weekend day? Did your parent date at that age? Did your parent have a job? Along the same lines, write a biographical sketch of one of your grandparents at your age. In both sketches, try to answer this question: In spite of all the changes in these persons' lives, in what ways are they the same persons today they were twenty or forty years ago?

2) Recall your first real friendship and write a paragraph about it, answering the following questions: What was the person's name? What was he or she like? How long were you friends? Are you still friends today? Why? Why not? What do you know about that person today?

Relationships 3
Reflect Values

The '80s and "ME"

The strength of our relationships is based heavily upon the values we choose to live by. And while we do not need to fear change in itself, we do need to look critically at how changes in society affect our values.

Recently on the front page of a major newspaper, a large headline ran across the top of the page:

THE KEY WORD FOR THE '80s IS "ME"!

This theme, the article explained, was the basis of a planning meeting attended by the heads of some of the nation's largest merchandising corporations. Consumers in the eighties, they felt, will be pursuing a self-image and a lifestyle based on the belief that "I am what I buy."

People will be willing to give up everything possible except their "ego-purchases," said a vice-president of the area's largest retailing corporation. "Non-ego" purchases, he continued, are things people need. But ego-products reveal lifestyles, promise an experience or happiness. They are symbols of our goals and what we value: skis mean Aspen, jogging shoes mean health, a fine leather briefcase means business success, a recreation vehicle means mobility, a cabin cruiser means leisure, and so on.

Clearly, as these planners see it, the "I am what I buy" belief reflects

lifestyle and living habits in our society. Are they right? Do we center our lives around purchases? Do we find our identity in a consumer lifestyle? Are we as tied to our consumer lifestyle as some business leaders believe?

Try this quiz to see if it answers any of these questions (Note: the term "free time" is time available outside of classes, homework, and necessary family obligations):

---

1) How much of my free time do I spend with others because I enjoy being with them? How much time do I spend doing hobbies I enjoy?
2) Do I have a job? If so, why do I want to earn money?
3) How much of my free time does the job take?
4) What percentage of my wages do I save? For what?
5) In the last two months what did I spend money on?
6) How can I describe the purposes of these purchases?
   a) necessity (non-ego purchases)
   b) non-essential (ego purchases)
   Fit both types of purchases into the following categories:
   a) for personal pleasure related to hobbies or interests
   b) for self-esteem
   c) for convention ("Everybody else has it.")
   d) so I could enjoy life more, be happy
7) What are the most pleasurable moments in my life?
8) How many of them are connected to goods or services I purchased?
9) After graduation, what are my goals in life? career goals? income goals? relationship goals? community goals?
10) Which of these goals are most essential for my happiness?
11) If suddenly I learned that someone would provide me with all of my basic *necessities* of life (food, clothing, shelter, transportation, education) but that I could have no money to buy any other consumer goods or services, what would be left that makes me happy in life?

The business planners mentioned earlier believe that most of the good feelings you have about yourself, about living with others, and about your life, relate to your consumer habits. Were they right?

Consumer Relationships

In recent years people who study American life have given a lot of thought to the effect of "spending" on our lives. Some concluded that even our relationships mirror our economic values. But before we talk about it, let's review the economic principles shared by many industrial nations.

Do you remember what you learned in grade school about the free enterprise or competitive system? What principles made "the good life" possible? Did you ever hear a coach explain that competition in sports is a good preparation for life? He or she was referring to qualities basic to the "free enterprise" system. And somewhere along the line you probably learned that:

1) **Our society was built by the spirit of independence and rugged individualism; and "pulling yourself up by your own bootstraps" is possible for everyone and is the mark of true success.**
2) **Success, esteem, and security is built by the spirit of competition, by gaining mastery, and by control of people and situations.**
3) **Success is measurable and often can be counted in dollars and cents.**
4) **We need and deserve rewards for what we do. There are no limits to the number of rewards for us if we work hard enough. The freedom to pursue and gain them is what brings the good life.**
5) **Society's growth is calculated in profits made, in goods and services sold (not in the quality of our lives, relationships, environment, or community life).**

Some researchers think the changes in family life today reflect more than anything else the economic values which we have learned to live by, values which underlie our political and social institutions. These values are underlying themes of our culture.

We are also shaped in our lives and in our relationships by an advertising technology which constantly creates new wants and desires. Historian John Edwards listed the effects of this technology on us as individuals:

1) As advertising pushes us to each new want, a little more self-control is destroyed.
2) It builds in the notion of "no-limits" to what we can and should enjoy.
3) It underlies an emphasis on the monetary worth of everything.
4) It builds in a need to connect tangible rewards to whatever we do.

This search for tangible rewards and unlimited satisfaction affects even our most intimate relationships of love, marriage, and parenting. This search, explained Edwards, causes serious problems in these relationships, as evidenced by the harsh ways in which our society treats children and the elderly—people who are too young or too old to furnish us with the great immediate rewards we seek. Both the young and the old are frequently resented for their dependency, rather than admired for their potential or experience.

Or look at the search for rewards in our dating system, repeated to the point that, by marriage, couples measure happiness that way, loving one another for the rewards. Studies show that, when problems arise and relationships no longer mean continuous rewarding, they become weakened. Couples who marry with a "consumer" mentality do not seem prepared for the giving required to keep marriages alive and growing.

A few years ago at the University of Massachusetts, some scholars came together for a symposium on "close relationships." Their papers include comments on intimacy which follow along this same line of discussion. Our society, psychologist Elizabeth Douvan explained, teaches us to have a "free-lunch" notion about our lives. This notion presumes that our individual choices do not hurt others, that natural resources do not get used up, that our actions do not cause events. Moreover, in a search for personal fulfillment we have the right to abandon commitments.

Another psychologist, Howard Gadlin, went further: he felt that our technological society teaches us to view sexual relationships as another technology. Sexual pleasure is seen as an item to enjoy, to become skilled at, to develop techniques for. Sex has become separated from our relationships, like a product to use and enjoy. Indeed, this researcher concluded, we learn to be **consumers of people** in our consumer society. We value others to the degree to which they can satisfy our needs. If we take Gadlin's point a step further, we might call these kinds of relationships **consumer relationships.**

Sometimes when we read ideas like these, it seems depressing: none of us likes to think that we are as programmed for unhappiness as the ideas suggest. But we should not feel this way. Reading such things can free us—by helping us avoid mistakes in our relationships. We all know that for many people relationships fail, sometimes miserably. That is depressing! But learning **why** many relationships self-destruct offers us a clear hope.

Consumer relationships, then, have built-in weaknesses:

1) "Dependency"-type relationships are formed when we depend too much on the other person to fill our needs for happiness, self-esteem, pride, career, or whatever.

2) Dependency-type relationships do not allow us to get to know the other person except in the ways he or she makes us happy or meets our needs. Because we do not know the other person on a more personal level, there will be a low level of trust, and it will be much harder to develop good communication.

3) In consumer relationships, it is difficult to make a commitment which survives change and time, because such a commitment requires much giving as well as taking. Enduring relationships cannot be built on the economic principle of getting as much as possible and giving as little as possible—not if they are to last, to survive time, trouble, and change.

4) Consumer relationships are immature because they reflect the "getting" aspect of children's relationships more than the "giving" quality of adult love.

Nurturing Relationships

Strong and satisfying relationships spring from a set of values different from "consumer" values. We can get a clue to what these values might be by asking ourselves some questions: What kind of people do you most enjoy being with? Have you ever felt very happy being with someone, and later wondered what made being with that person seem

so good? Do you ever feel that "When I'm with that person I can really be myself"?

These clues point mainly to the need in each of us **to find out who we are and to become that person.** Becoming "ourselves" takes a long time. It is, we have said already, a process of growing, of discovery. It happens gradually through the years and most of all through the relationships we form with others.

Can you remember your best friends in grade school? in junior high? in tenth grade? Were they the same people? Are they still your good friends? Probably not, because you have changed since then. Through those friendships you discovered things you liked and did not like in others. Probably you now like being with people who are different from the people you liked being with a few years ago.

Each friendship taught you about yourself. You developed new interests and talents. And you expanded your hopes for yourself and others. Friendships which reveal these things to us help us grow. Real friendships are those that helped you be more the person you would like to be.

Real friendships nurture us. What does it mean to nurture? A mother and father who give their loving care to an infant are nurturing that infant. When you nurture another you are being open to, supporting, and enjoying the healthy growth of that person. You are involved, becoming more generous, learning more about yourself, feeling good about growing by giving as well as getting. In nurturing relationships, good things happen to both persons involved.

Yet nurturing relationships do not refer only to infant/parent relationships. They happen at any age. Real friendships are nurturing relationships. Any two people who support and enjoy one another have a nurturing relationship. A husband and wife in a good marriage—who are really friends—have a nurturing relationship.

To describe nurturing relationships we can say:

---

1) They are the shared experiences of two or more people, each trying to be open to the growth and happiness of the other. Obviously, in relationships between adults, the openness of one can be more closely equal to that of the other than in infant/parent relationships.

2) They bring satisfaction, mutual growth, and pleasure to both persons involved.

3) They become stronger in time and through change because they build up a shared history of good experiences: joy in bringing happiness to the other, gratitude for good things received, admiration for the good qualities of the other, need for the mutual support, care, understanding of problems faced by one another.

4) Nurturing relationships allow people to make a commitment to one another.

To sum it all up, we could say that **when we are talking about nurturing relationships, we are talking about love.**

Why use the word **nurturing,** however, if actually we are talking about **love?** A quick answer might be that the word **love** is so often misused and overused that it is not of much help any more.

A better answer is found in a suggestion someone once made about "love talk." It was suggested that if Eskimos have fifty-two different names for snow because it is so important to their lives, then we should have at least that many words for love. The fact is we need a lot of words to describe all the kinds and qualities of love.

Nurturing is a good term to use for love because it carries along with it the ideas of life and growth and giving. We nurture live things, helping them to grow, giving them food, warmth, care, whatever it takes. In short, nurturing suggests the aspects of love which are integral to the concept of love in Christian faith.

Christian Faith and Love

This course will have to deal with the limitations and barriers which impede love, like the pressures of our consumer society described already. What, then, is the "rock" on which we can build good friendships, nurturing relationships?

For Christians, the answer is clearly found in the life and teachings of Jesus. In his life, Jesus broke through many of the barriers to love which often limit us in our relationships—selfishness, fear, prejudice, resentment. Rather than possessing others, he proclaimed loving others as the greatest commandment, and he lived a life committed to being of service to others.

In the gospel accounts of his public ministry, short-lived as it was, we are told that Jesus loved and cared for anyone—the sick, the poor,

the foreigner, the tax-collector, anyone who needed it. In other words, there were **no restrictions** to whom or how much he could love:

"You shall love your neighbor as yourself . . . "

And Jesus' idea of neighbor was anyone "nigh" or near, anyone he met—without exception.

We also read that Jesus was condemned to die for teaching and defending the helpless and forgotten people in his society. He died willingly to prove those principles of love which seem hopelessly unreasonable: to have love, you must give it away—**no conditions, no rewards.** And to find yourself, you must give yourself to others.

And he took the bread, and when he had given thanks he broke it and gave it to them, saying, "This is my body which is given for you."

For people who believe in Jesus' Resurrection, all the remaining questions about love's power are answered by that event in which nothing, not even death, cancelled love.

"Wherever two or more are gathered together in my name, there I am, in the midst of them."

Jesus took the lid off love; there are **no time limits and no physical limits** to his relationships.

"I will be with you all days even to the end of the world."

The key to our own understanding of love in Christian faith begins with this last point. **Belief in the Resurrection teaches us that love—not rewards, not success, not wealth, not competition—is the guiding principle of life.** The gospel could not be clearer on this point: "God is love." As Christians, then, we are freed from the belief that our lives are governed by the laws of the "survival of the fittest," that our own well-being must be bought at someone else's expense. Instead we are invited to replace selfishness, fear, prejudices, and envy with marvelous human values including trust, honesty, cooperation, and ability to love with commitment.

From Jesus' decision to die for love of people, we also learn that our identity and our growth is grounded as much in our **giving re-lationships** as it is in our individual survival. As Christians, then, we are called to give ourselves fearlessly in our relationships, to make **commitments to intimacy.** Much of this course will deal with what this intimacy means in our relationships.

Finally, Jesus' life teaches us that love is pursued not only in the few intense, intimate relationships we develop, but also in daily, ordinary encounters with all kinds of people. As Christians, then, we are called to nurture others by making **commitments to service.** Usually these are commitments to careers and lifestyles which promote justice—supporting dignity and protecting life.

It is this example of the life of Jesus which provides the basis on which relationships will last through the years just ahead. For today, the entire human family faces many changes and challenges.

Remember, Relationships Are Processes

To summarize all that we have said about consumer and nurturing relationships, it might be a good idea to use a chart. The following one suggests some of the traits of the two relationships. None of our relationships, it should be said first, is **completely** a consumer or a nurturing relationship. We have many kinds of relationships in our lives. Some are more of the nurturing sort and others are more selfish than supportive. The important question is: In which direction is each of our relationships headed?

CONSUMER RELATIONSHIPS	NURTURING RELATIONSHIPS
selfish	giving, sharing
demanding	patient
indifferent to others	kind, caring, warm to others
untrusting	trusting
plotting, manipulative	joyful, spontaneous, honest
fearful, holding back	hopeful
centered on rewards	centered on growth and giving
controlled, limited involvement	willing to risk, able to change
short-term	enduring, lasting

FOR REVIEW

1) Define what is meant by a "free-lunch" notion of life.

2) Define consumer relationships.

3) Describe what is meant by nurturing relationships.

4) What was Jesus' understanding of love as we know it?

5) What two kinds of commitments does Christian faith challenge people to make?

FOR REFLECTION

1) Answer the questions on page 29 in writing. Then, list under the heading SELF GROWTH some ways in which you might better spend your time and money on your real interests. Under the heading FRIENDSHIP, list some ways in which you might better spend your time and money on people you care about.

2) Write a story about consumer and nurturing relationships using as many of the following characters and items as possible: you, a friend of yours, Ebenezer Scrooge, your favorite sport, a hundred dollar bill, a remarkable day, your city or town.

Building 4
Love Relationships

Looking for Closeness in Our Lives

Recently, two writers collaborated on a book called **Relationships**, interviewing 300 couples in the course of their research. "Everyone," said one of the co-authors in summary, "is looking for a close, one-to-one relationship." However making such relationships last is difficult today, because, the authors concluded, people have the freedom to choose relationships other than lifelong marriage.

What did the authors mean by a "close" relationship? a "one-to-one" relationship? One of the first things we run into when we talk about relationships is the fact that the word means different things to different people. Our understanding of what **relationship** means depends on our experiences and our expectations of relationship.

For many people **relationship** means just one thing—a sexual relationship. For example, the "personal" column of a local weekly music and entertainment publication recently listed 129 ads, and most of them were requesting correspondence from people interested in "relationships." One of them read like this:

SWM exec., early 30's and generous, seeks SWF 'sweet young thing' (pref. under 21) for intimate relationship. Should be pretty, submissive, and discreet. Good times, travel, and other goodies inc. poss. allowance. No problem types, please. Send photo (a must) and letter w/phone to Uncle . . .

What did "Uncle" mean by **relationship** and **intimate?** How many other meanings can you list for these words? When we form relationships today, it is important that we go far beyond the physical in understanding what a good human relationship can be.

Each of us has experienced different levels of relationship. Sometimes it is hard to know what a close relationship—a nurturing friendship—really is. Here is a mental exercise which helps us stand back from our relationships:

Suppose someone were to say to you, "Here's a truckload of hats—each one different for each type of relationship you have with another person." How many hats would you take?

You would need one hat to wear when you were with your parents, possibly one hat for each parent. You would need a hat to wear with your brothers and sisters, possibly a different hat for each one. The same would be true for your relatives and neighbors.

You would probably take several hats to wear to school: certain hats for your friends, certain ones for teachers, special hats for special friends and special teachers.

Soon you would find yourself distinguishing types of friends ranging from acquaintances to the one or two with whom you are very close—if you are very close with anyone. If you are lucky, you would have a hat for a friend with whom you feel able to be "completely yourself." You would find this hat to be a very special hat—probably one of your favorites.

Your need for hats would increase if you have a job, although you might wear the same hat with your boss that you wear with some teachers, and the same hat you chose for certain friends might work for some of your co-workers.

Eventually you would distinguish certain hats as "authority" hats, "good time" hats, "interesting conversation" hats, "son or daughter" hats, "sports fan" hats, "good friends" hats, and so on. In effect, you would find yourself distinguishing the different ways you relate to other persons in your life.

And if the supplier of hats had given all of your friends the same instructions, you would come to see that others needed larger or smaller numbers of hats than you did. The person with the least number of hats would show either remarkable freedom

or a lot of limits in most of his or her relationships. If the hat worn most of the time were the "I can be completely myself" hat, that would indeed be a fortunate and happy person.

It is this freedom to "be ourselves" that makes a relationship close. Most of us hide our real selves, or some aspects of our real selves, in various habits or patterns we learned early in our lives. Sometimes this is conscious, but most often it is the unconscious ways we react to others that block intimacy in our lives and prevent us from becoming or staying very close to another.

Developing Intimacy

A doctor who works with couples who have sexual problems said that intimacy is "the mutual belief of two people that what is hidden between them hurts their relationship, and what is revealed between them can only help their relationship." Can you think of a better definition?

The greater the degree of friendship, the greater the degree of trust, acceptance, freedom to be oneself, love for the person of the other, assumption of responsibility for one another, and respect. Good friendship accepts the other person as he or she really is, not as what each **needs** and **wants** the other to be. Good friendship is nurturing: it allows each person to be oneself, to be loved for that, and therefore gives support for that person to continue to grow in becoming the person he or she needs to be.

We have said that close relationships are those in which we can "be ourselves." But how does this kind of friendship happen? Think of a good friend you have had. Certainly when you first met, you did not feel that complete openness to be yourself. You might even have disliked that person because of your own barriers to intimacy. "She must be stuck-up—she carries herself like she's too good for everybody else!" or "He really talks as though he's God's gift to others." But when you got to know that person, you realized you were mistaken.

To become close, there was a certain process you went through: one of you had to make a first move, taking a risk to be friends, revealing oneself a little bit—perhaps even feeling a little foolish; the other responded in friendliness and not rejection, and a little trust was established between the two of you.

That good friendship really grew through a series of risk-takings and acceptances—where one of you revealed a little more about your own feelings and thoughts, and the other person accepted you. Trust grew, enough so that one of you could begin to reveal even more, only to find acceptance once again. This process continued until each began to feel that "I can really be myself with you." Does this describe any experience you have had with another person?

Intimacy between two persons—and we use the word in a psychological, emotional sense, not the physical, sexual sense—is a very special kind of good friendship. We need intimacy, but intimacy is rarely total and complete. We work at it. We possess it by degrees. If we find great intimacy with one person, we are indeed fortunate.

Keeping Intimacy

When we find good friendship, it is not easy to keep it in today's world. How do we keep it? How do we build intimacy as we grow and change through time? As we discussed in the last chapter, the critical tension in building intimacy today is the conflict people face between seeking personal fulfillment and maintaining close relationships.

It is a tension between how much "me-ness" and "we-ness" shall exist in our relationships. If relationships are to last, as we discussed earlier, they have to be part of our personal fulfillment, not something that hurts our growth. Yet one of the difficulties in building relationships today is that we learn to see "giving" as somehow hurting our own needs for personal growth.

Secondly, most people think about marriage or intimacy as something we can find and then keep—like a beautiful house we find, move into, and live in happily ever after. We learn to think of close relationships like some kind of destination we arrive at with another.

Close relationships are not "found": there is no such thing as a permanent state of intimacy. As Carl Rogers described it, the "good life" is a process of being, not a state of being. Relationships are also this. The "process of intimacy," if we can call it that, consists of habits of openness, acceptance, trust, revelation with another—habits which we must continue to work at if love is to stay alive and to grow.

Talk, acceptance, trust, and ultimately commitment are actual tools, links, that keep two persons close as they travel together through personal and social change. Intimacy can grow with these tools if the relationship is giving. Intimacy cannot exist in relationships that are primarily needing, looking to the other for rewards—that is, consumer types of relationships.

Communication—
The Primary Skill for Building Intimacy

Virginia Satir, a leader in the field of family therapy, has written and spoken about relationships with profound insight. It is communication, she wrote, that is the largest single factor which affects the kinds of relationships we make with one another—a gauge by which two people can measure each other's feelings of self-worth, a tool by which each can deepen self-worth.

In her book **Peoplemaking**, she explains that each of us is constantly communicating both verbally and non-verbally with others as we transmit our ideas and feelings in our family relationships.

Only one type of communication is acceptable, however: the type that "nurtures." Nurturing communication builds trust. It is the kind that occurs when we "level" with another, telling that person what we actually feel inside.

Most people do not communicate this way. Most of us did not learn to "level" with others in our own personal history. Usually we learned a "family style" of communication, and we continue to use it in the relationships we build later in life. Most often we learned to use "double-message" communication: our words say one thing while our bodies reveal another.

We cannot hide our feelings, Satir says. Even when we try to hide them in the words we say, those feelings come out through our bodies, voice, face, eyes. And it is our feelings, she believes, that are all too often wrongly interpreted by others.

Other persons read our double-messages according to their own level of self-worth. We can feel criticism, for example, in something another says, if we are expecting criticism. Yet that person might never have intended it. On the contrary, he or she might have been feeling fatigue, fear, indecision, self-doubt, fear of our own reaction—or none of those things.

Can you think of examples when a friend said something to you which you took—by the **way** he or she said it—as criticism, only to find out later that your friend was surprised to learn you felt that way?

Satir identifies and describes several kinds of "double-message communication"—habitual ways of talking which sow distrust between husband and wife, friends, or lovers who are then forced (1) to choose between each other's words or their non-word messages, or (2) to ignore both, or (3) to accept both. None of these choices promotes trust or growth.

To build intimacy, then, we need to learn to discover ways to change patterns of communicating, to find more nurturing ways to talk and act with persons.

As part of this, we also have to try to accept ourselves in our own inadequacies—enough so that we can be open to criticism of our own "style" of communicating. It means being able to take risks in our friendships, becoming more open and honest with persons we care about. It means continuing this honesty as we change through the years.

This "levelling" in communication, as Satir calls it, is essential to forming and keeping nurturing relationships. **Communication which reveals our true feelings is our most effective way of building trust with another.** It involves taking a risk: the person we care about might not like us. But a self risked and accepted becomes able to take even greater risks the next time. Strangely, this willingness to risk in a relationship is the very key to staying close. **It is through this process that we grow in knowledge of another, and in acceptance of our own self-worth.** When we feel understood and accepted, we feel free to love generously. In return, our "love need" is richly filled.

Barriers to Intimacy

In her writings on people's relationships, psychiatrist Irene Kassorla says that most of her patients' ability to fall in love and stay in love is limited by a thing called "distance" which all of us learn early in life. The way each of us "distances" himself or herself from others varies, depending on the causes. Sometimes we close ourselves off because we fear rejection or being hurt. Other times we are living out **barriers to intimacy** we learned from our family. "When we feel we are getting too close, we find ways to separate—to stop the love and pleasure in our lives, and to subconsciously sabotage the 'intimate moment,' " she wrote.

In addition, Kassorla believes, we all enter into relationships using our family's style of handling communication and ways of being close to another. We look for friends and lovers with similar emotional training, she believes, and "subconsciously" we look for this in our experiences even on a first date.

Do you remember the "time-machine" used in chapter 1? Again move backward in time and think of values and feelings you learned growing up in your family. For instance, can you make friends equally well with men and women your age? What is your idea of a good friendship? What are the qualities you look for in someone you have as a friend? Can you trace any of them to traits you learned to admire in your own family life?

Here is an example of how traits we acquire in our early years can influence our relationships. How would you describe this boy's emotional training?

A teacher in a boy's high school was discussing relationships with a small group of seniors. They had been discussing the kinds of relationships they establish with others and were probing the extent to which feelings learned early in life affected those relationships. The teacher asked the boys to try an experiment.

"Relax," he said. "Close your eyes, and try to take yourselves back to your earliest childhood memories. Take time, and try to remember an experience—when you were very small—that hurt you. Try to feel the feelings you felt then. If you can't really remember such an experience, make up one you think probably happened and how you probably felt.

"Do you remember a feeling of sadness? loneliness? anger?" he continued. "Was it fear or hatred?"

The group sat in silence. Some stared into space; others sat with their eyes closed. It was obvious that some were grasping for the bits of memory and feelings they sensed were in their past.

"Now," he said, "compose what you remembered into a story about a three year old child—who is really you—and tell it to us. If you haven't been able to remember anything, make it up and tell us."

After a pause, a student named John offered to share what he really remembered. "I was in the kitchen with my mother," he said. "My father had left home a few days earlier. I asked my mother, 'Where's Daddy?' "

"He's gone," she said.

"Is he coming back?"

"No." At that point the teacher asked John what he had been feeling when his mother said that.

"First hurt," said John. "Then resentment."

"How do you feel about him now?"

John hesitated for a minute and looked away as he said, "I hate him. I don't ever see him. I'm angry, resentful. And sometimes I think that every day that hatred grows deeper."

There was silence in the room. Everyone knew it was a tense

moment for John when the teacher asked him, "How do you relate to people now? Do these feelings for your father affect the way you respond to people you know now?"

John looked directly at the teacher as he answered, "I don't let people get close to me."

The eyes of the teacher relayed to John the compassion he felt for him as he said, "You know, John, past events and whether they have good or bad effects on us really all depend on what we do with them. Once you forgive your dad, John, you'll learn people can leave you and you'll still be OK."

Not all of us are fortunate enough to experience as far-reaching a self-discovery as John had that day. To that teacher, forgiveness on John's part would be the act of choosing again to relate. That particular moment of self-discovery only came after a sensitive and caring teacher was able to bring John to a point where he could take some risks in revealing his feelings.

But to bring John to that point, that teacher had taken similar risks in his own personal openness and honesty—which he brought to the classroom. Clearly, that teacher must have "levelled" many times with John. He had built a level of trust which gave John the support he needed to bare his own feelings—enough to discover how he was creating "distance" in his own life.

Each of us has our own learned patterns of reacting to others, our own attitudes toward being close. Remember what we said about our "personal history" in the first chapter? Through our early experiences we learned and chose these patterns of acting because they "worked" for us at earlier times in our lives.

Stereotyped ways of acting or communicating are also barriers to intimacy. For example, in his book, **Games People Play**, Dr. Eric Berne describes stereotyped ways of relating which people learn. **Games** are a substitute for intimacy, says Berne, and when we "play" them we obscure what is really happening between two people. Games are fixed mental sets we learn, he says, in which we interpret another's words, expressions, or actions as we have learned to expect or want that person to act toward us.

How do you know when you are "game playing"? He suggests you ask yourself: Where is your mind when your body is in a certain encounter? How well is your mind perceiving what is happening?

For example, supposing you were to give a report to a group of students and teachers tomorrow, but could not feel comfortable about having to do this—your confidence, your self-image was on the line, you felt. You might unconsciously react in one of three basic "game" patterns:

3

---

1) You could be overly fearful—so preoccupied with how you will perform, how they will react, that this takes over your thoughts. As you face everyone, you hear in your mind the thoughts you fear the audience is having about your performance.

2) You might be thinking of excuses for not doing well, irritation at having to make this report—or probably welcoming excuses that "it was too hard to do well anyway" or "I'm glad the library was closed and I couldn't get the books I needed."

3) Or you might be focusing on yourself, conscious only of your own words, your actions, how you stand, hold the mike, the tone of your voice, whether you breathe fast, clear your throat too much, what expression is on your face. This limited focus prevents you from knowing what is really happening between you and the audience.

Our goal should always be to be comfortable enough with ourselves that we are free to live in the present—not controlled by some imaginary obstacles, residues from our childhood, reactions from the past. Persons who are fully alive are open to and aware of what is happening between themselves and other persons.

Consumer Relationships—Barriers to Friendship

To the list of barriers to intimacy, we can add consumer relationships—relationships in which we value another person primarily for the rewards he or she gives us. In consumer relationships—as we discussed them in chapter 3—we see persons as a **means** to an end, a means to our own personal pleasure and good feelings of self-worth.

Naturally, some of this is present in all of our relationships; but when it exists to such a degree that we cannot go beyond the "getting" to the "giving," we have erected a barrier to real friendship. A self-centered approach to relationships works against intimacy because we fear learning things about another which might be different from what we expect from them, or hurtful to our own self-image.

This chapter opened by noting that we are each looking for a close, one-to-one relationship. We then discussed tools or skills which help build loving relationships. In addition, in order to form strong friendships and to build intimacy, we have seen that we need to be aware of the unconscious ways we erect barriers to both. Yet it would be a mistake to think that we must be or even could be **totally** open to **every** friend. Separateness, a sense of privacy, is also a human need. Each one of us is a unique person, a separate individual, living essentially alone. No one person can—or should—know all our thoughts or feelings.

So far, this course has dealt with the needs and issues confronting all of us in our search for intimacy and love. In the next chapters, we will examine how our sexuality—our being male or female—also influences our identity and our relationships.

FOR REVIEW

    1) **Define intimacy.**

    2) **What is meant by "levelling"?**

    3) **Give examples from your own life of the kinds of "games" mentioned in the text.**

FOR REFLECTION

    1) **Write a newspaper ad of about fifty words asking for letters from people you might want as friends. (Try to answer the question: What does the word *relationship* mean to you?)**

    2) **To gain a clearer idea of the many relationships surrounding you at present, draw a group of circles representing the members of your family, including grandparents or anyone who is absent. Draw *two arrows* between *each* of the circles—one to indicate, for example, that you are a daughter to your mother and another going in the opposite direction to indicate that she is a mother to you. If you come from a family of five persons, then, you will need twenty arrows to represent all of the relationships. Then, somewhere near your circle, add circles to represent your closest friends and, when appropriate, connect these with arrows.**

Our Sexual Selves 5

SEX is a household word these days. How many films have you seen which show the leading characters tumbling into bed together? How many quiz and comedy shows can you list whose humor leans toward sex? How often do you see magazines and newspapers print articles detailing the sleep-in arrangements of famous people?

The following topics would easily fit into the regular format of many leading magazines and newspapers: "sex and teenagers," "marriage and a happy sex-life," "single and sexy," "the middle years and sexual fulfillment," and "sex after sixty?"

Do you agree that we live in a sexually "turned-on" society?

It was not always this way. We have had what many term a "sexual revolution." This great change has led to sharp differences in Americans' attitudes about sexuality and sex. As a result, there are many mixed messages about the role of sex in our relationships.

This is a chapter about sex and sexuality. When we talk about sex in these pages, we are talking about sex as a genital function—its physical expression and those acts that immediately lead up to it. Sex, in this sense, is only one part of who we are. It is different from our sexuality. "**Sex,**" someone once said, "is something we do. **Sexuality** is who we are." **Sex** is one way we express physically our relationship with another person. Our **sexuality** means who we are, how we view our-

selves as particular men or women. **Sex** is related to reproduction, to creating new life. It should be a very pleasurable emotional experience, which draws a man and a woman together. **Sexuality** involves our whole self—intellectual, emotional, spiritual—our masculine or feminine role, our capacity for friendship, relationship, intimacy.

Conflicting Messages Shape Our Attitudes

Do you remember the stories of the wild children? They reminded us that we are shaped—even made human—by the world into which we are born. The attitudes of those around us affect us profoundly. Society teaches us certain attitudes about sex and sexuality. One such message-bearer is television. Would you be surprised to learn that the National Federation of Decency reported that monitoring 762 hours of prime-time programming of three major TV networks revealed that 88 percent of all sexual encounters were portrayed outside of marriage?

Another message we get from TV stresses sexual technique. We often hear that sexual "expertise" is essential if a marriage is to begin happily. Many young adults enter marriage today unaware that a tender, loving person is the ultimate arousal, not sexual skill. Some come to fear marriage because they overestimate the importance of sexual expertise.

Another kind of message, what one teenage counselor termed "permission giving," reaches all of us through the media. She explained it this way: anyone watching an actor and actress fall into bed sees clothes fall off, sees everything approved, sees everything perfect—often without problems, without fear of pregnancy, without any connection to an ongoing relationship. Films, television, and books give "permission" for premarital sexual experiences, but they are experiences disconnected from real relationships and real life.

Another message source is music. "I can think of one record," said a nurse who works with teenagers, "describing that this night is the night to make love and how it feels. I can think of another about the woman who is giving birth to his baby. Nothing in these is related to relationships. None of these tell kids that sexual feelings aren't the same as being in love. The film, music, and print media are molding our culture," she continued, "and no one really tells kids anything very different."

The "double standard" is also a message we receive. This message is an old one. In one form or another, it has existed for many centuries, and it reigned supreme in the Victorian Era in the last century, holding a strong grip on people's lives. During that time "good" women could not enjoy sexual experiences. Wives were expected to tolerate sex, but not to enjoy it. There was little public understanding of the goodness of sex in a loving relationship.

A double standard of **sexual license** for men and **sexual restraint** for women became firmly entrenched in many cultural groups. Right along with it were matching masculine and feminine roles, encouraging men to gain sexual expertise before marriage since, it was assumed, men were responsible for any sexual enjoyment women experienced. As part of this double standard, prostitutes, then as now, faced prosecution and condemnation, while their customers were condoned or ignored.

All things considered, we live in a nation of mixed messages about sex. Underlying them all is a popular view which sees sex as bad, something which should not exist in good relationships. What else would account for the existence of sex as the basis of multi-million-dollar industries—such as prostitution and pornographic book, maga-

zine, and film industries? Sex, disconnected from relationships, is a commodity to be purchased, or something to bargain over during a date. In short, sex often is separated from love and good friendship and is, instead, a consumer item.

Growing up in this setting is not easy. We live in a contradictory world of "sex is all good, but it's really bad." In the transition to adulthood, it is often hard for a person to know what is right. Teenagers, who especially need love, acceptance, and emotional security, often feel the conflicting pressures behind these messages about sexuality.

The various messages have their effects. For example, a young man wrote to Ann Landers not long ago, saying he felt like some kind of "freak" because he was still a virgin. A ninth grader recently talked about the effects of TV and film media. "You can't help but get the feeling," he said, "that sex may not be right, but it is inevitable before adulthood. You get the idea that almost everyone is sleeping around." What he also could have said is that it is easy to conclude that "sex may not be right, but it is acceptable."

The pressures of our sexually turned-on society are producing dramatic results: today studies and statistics indicate more premarital sexual activity and teenage pregnancies than ever before in our history. There is an epidemic of teenage pregnancies today, particularly between the ages of fifteen and nineteen. Some say percentages have actually increased; others that they are no different than earlier years, but the numbers astound because of the large number of teens and young adults in our society.

A statistical sampling looks something like this:

---

*There are 600,000 teenage mothers each year.

*Between the 1960s and early 1970s the percentage of out-of-wedlock births to teenage mothers doubled.

*Three in five pregnant teenage brides are divorced in six years.

*Of 21 million young persons between ages 15 and 19, more than half—11 million—are estimated to have had sexual intercourse (7 million young men and 4 million young women).

*One-fifth of 8 million 13 and 14 year-olds are believed to have had intercourse.

In any case, large numbers of teenagers have chosen to be sexually active. Yet there is very little public recognition of this fact. In our schools and families there is little open discussion about sexual feelings, or about the place of sex in relationships. Many young persons live with a "communication black-out" on the role of sex in their relationships. Studies show that most young persons prefer to receive sex education from parents, but that actually the main sources of information are friends, schools, and the popular media.

As a result it is easy to pick up confused ideas about sex. For example, have you ever felt you were receiving any of the following messages?

"Sex in itself is wrong; save it for the person you love."
(Indirectly you may be hearing that sex is "dirty.")

"Sex is good, but that's all I'll ever say about it."
(Indirectly you might be picking up the message that sex is too bad to talk about.)

> **"Men should be experienced in sex before marriage."**
> **(Indirectly you might be picking up the messages that there is a double-standard, that men and women need not live by the same moral standards, that experience is necessary for a happy sexual relationship in marriage.)**

Although we receive many mixed messages about sex and sexuality, there are no longer any strong cultural values regarding premarital sex. Given that fact, and with little open discussion within families about sex, many young people face a confusing time shaping their personal values. The remainder of this chapter, then, will attempt to explain briefly our physical and emotional development as well as offer some guidelines for a practical moral stance regarding sex.

Understanding Our Physical Development

Today teenagers often become physically mature at ages eleven and twelve—ten years before reaching independence in our society. (Girls previously began menstruation later, at the average age of sixteen in 1795.) This phase of your own physical development is complete by this time, but it is important to review to get a perspective on your other needs.

With the onset of puberty in young men, glands produce the hormones which affect growth in genital development and in related body characteristics. The voice changes; hair begins to grow in underarm and pubic areas; testicles and penis become mature sizes. Hormonal production stimulates sperm production in the testicles, occasionally passing out of the penis in "wet dreams" or normal, spontaneous nocturnal dreams.

The sexual drive is strong in male teenagers. Experts say it is so strong that it reaches a lifetime peak in intensity between ages seventeen and twenty-one. It is entirely natural for young men to be stimulated merely by a picture, a touch, a thought. A sexually turned-on society makes it all the more difficult for many young men to live without acting on these natural feelings.

Males can be aroused by less stimulation than females; in addition, male arousal can happen much faster. One anthropologist, Paul Bohanon, describes it this way: the sexual drive in the male is not stronger, but full arousal in the male may be a matter of only a few seconds, whereas it is almost always a matter of several minutes in the female.

Each sex should not think that the other's sexual responses "work like their own," continues Bohanon. Men's genitals—their location being more external than the female's—need protection and become a matter of greater awareness since they are subject to more frequent stimulation in the course of normal activities. Women, physically so different, are usually not aware of the "constancy of the sexual pressures" on the males.

It is important to understand how frequently, and how naturally, males especially can feel sex arousal. Women and men alike need to know that these feelings are good, natural, and all right to have—but not an indication of love or intimacy. As one teen counselor put it, "Kids really need to know that feeling 'horny' isn't being in love."

In girls, physical maturation begins with the development of breast buds, pubic hair, and the onset of menstruation—today as early as sixth or seventh grade. Once menstruation begins, for the next thirty or so years, the young girl's ovaries will function on a monthly cycle— ripening one of her fixed number of eggs and releasing it a few weeks prior to menstruation, when the uterus is prepared for the possibility of implantation of a fertilized egg.

If intercourse were to take place, only one of the millions of male sperm released with the semen is needed to fertilize an egg, which would then implant itself in the uterus. Many teenagers—even young adults—have little understanding of how easy it is to become pregnant, because they are unaware that sperm can swim to fertilize an egg even from the exterior of the woman's body, near the opening of the vagina. Many are also unaware that:

1) for pregnancy to occur, intercourse need not occur right at the time of ovulation (release of the egg),
2) sperm can live several days inside the Fallopian tubes,
3) the egg itself may live many hours after ovulation,
4) time of ovulation may vary greatly from one girl to another,
5) sexual position or frequency of intercourse or psychological attitude has nothing to do with whether a woman becomes pregnant.

Females are less easily aroused than males, most experts say, but when it happens arousal is just as strong. No one knows whether this difference is cultural or biological. There are always exceptions—as one doctor noted who runs a clinic which cares for thousands of teenagers each year, "It's not always the boys who are trying to change the girls' minds—there are girls who love to make love, take drugs to feel aroused, not knowing that drugs make sex less, not more . . ." Many researchers, however, have come to believe that women actually reach their peak in sexual drive in their thirties—and that a strong sexual drive lasts into their sixties.

It is important to remember that all of us are not walking examples of the researchers' model, but rather that members of a species have individual differences reaching across the entire spectrum, ranging from almost non-existent sexual feelings to strong, almost constant feelings, with the majority of us somewhere in the middle.

Understanding Our Emotional Development

Have you had overwhelming feelings of love for another person, that is, have you ever "fallen in love"? If you have, it is a wonderful experience you share with many people your age. "The ability to fall passionately in love is the most spectacular behavioral feature of adolescence," writes researcher Dr. John Money.

For some teenagers, these strong feelings, called **infatuation,** mark the first experience of "getting past self," in other words, being brought out of themselves with incredible feelings of caring for someone else. Infatuation can be an important step toward maturity because it can heighten our sensitivity to others.

If you have been infatuated with someone, you also know that infatuation is not merely sexual arousal or "horniness." Sexual arousal is a purely physical response seeking relief from bodily pressures and tensions. Someone who is infatuated, on the other hand, is not looking for relief but rather for greater and deeper knowledge of that other person—in other words, for intimacy.

The difference is seen just in the language we use. "Horny" language can be found in the pages of sex magazines, in jokes about body parts and their sizes. Someone who has "fallen in love," on the other hand, tends to find poetic language more suited to his or her marvelous, powerful emotions.

If you have ever wanted to write a poem to someone special, you understand the difference between sexual arousal and infatuation. Infatuation is a creative, life-loving urge. It has created not only great poetry but has also forged great love relationships. A love relationship can have no better beginning than in mutual feelings of infatuation.

Yet infatuation is just that—a start—because it has time limits. Research has shown that this state of intense feelings lasts about two years, characterized by an intense awareness of the loved one, an urgent need to be close, a yearning to touch and fondle. So if we are looking for a key to lasting love, we must look beyond—but not overlook—the part infatuation can play. By the time infatuation wears off, a couple must have worked toward a real friendship or nurturing love.

How is infatuation different from nurturing love? Infatuation is the experience of being drawn to another because of one's own needs, not the other's. The other is seen as someone who can complete us or make us whole. The problem is the other person might not agree or care nearly as much. While nurturing love is mutual, infatuation then can be totally one-sided. This is why, unfortunately, such relationships often come to a heart-breaking finish. A bittersweet poem titled "Warning" by Alice Walker describes this painful experience:

To love a man wholly
love him
feet first
> **head down**
> **eyes cold**
> **closed**
in depression.
It is too easy to love
a surfer
white eyes
godliness &
> **bronze**
in the bright sun.

Sexual Relationships Reflect Our Values

A recent **Newsweek** cover story on teenage sex carried a cartoon in which a boy says to his friend, "To tell the truth, I wish I'd been born back before sex." The mixed-up messages about sex we get from others along with the complicated emotions we experience as individuals can make sex seem threatening or at least confusing. This cartoon seems to express those feelings.

We do not want to cling to Victorian attitudes about sex. Sex brings joy, pleasure, completion, and strength to a committed love relationship. The more important question, then, is, "When does sex belong in a relationship?" As Christians, we also want to ask, "When is sex morally OK?"

Many people today have learned to distrust long-term love, much as they might need it and secretly want it. They may be unwilling, then, to admit to the importance of a permanent or an intimate sexual relationship. In that case, another question arises: "What role does sex play in a relationship that has neither intimacy nor commitment?" These questions need your personal reflection and some discussion.

First of all, how well do you know your own sexual values? Can you explain them? Here is an exercise which might help. Study this list of statements commonly directed at young persons. They are statements about sexual acts (acts of sexual intercourse or acts leading immediately to intercourse). Do you agree or disagree with each of the following statements?

Sexual acts are all right if they enhance your self-esteem.

Sexual acts are all right if they bring pleasure.

Sexual acts are all right if they are voluntary, that is, resulting from your personal decisions rather than decisions someone else makes for you.

Sexual acts are all right if they don't harm anyone, including you, the other person, or possibly an unwanted child. (The potential harm might be emotional, psychological, or physical— the spread of venereal disease.)

Sexual acts are all right if they express your real feelings.

Sexual acts are all right if they increase your capacity to trust, as well as your integrity, if they dissolve barriers between people and foster each person's zest for living.

Sexual acts are all right only in the intimacy of a marriage relationship.

Did you find that you could neither agree nor disagree with some of the statements? It is likely that you do not have clear answers to all of these statements because there are difficult questions hidden in them. Further, the actual reasons **why** teenagers have sex cannot be summed up in any one of these statements. We will now spend some time discussing these reasons as teenagers themselves and their counselors understand them. The list of reasons actually began with two factors we have already discussed—sexual arousal and infatuation. Both of these factors are healthy, inborn parts of our human development. In contrast, the reasons teenagers have sex, as described in the following sections, are special issues we face today as members of our culture.

Our Need for Touching

Have you ever dated or been attracted to someone whom you would not want as a friend? Quite often we view a person as a possible sexual partner without considering him or her first as a prospective friend.

What attracts us if it is not the person himself or herself? Is it his or her face, voice, body, talents, specific accomplishments?

Often, our feelings play a strong role in an attraction toward another—even if we know very little about the other as a person. Feelings can make us want to reach out, touch that person, hold them close, embrace. Feelings like this can be an expression of deep friendship or feelings can express something else. It is important to understand our feelings. Sometimes, feelings merely express our need for touch.

Each of us needs loving, caring touches. Touch, our most basic and earliest form of communication, told us as infants that we were loved, needed, and accepted. Our need for touch remains throughout our lives. Touch gives us a sense of our own self-worth.

Studies have pointed out our need for touch. For example, infant monkeys deprived of holding and cuddling and the feel of skin are unable to learn to mate as adults and become sexually disorganized. Their sexual training, the study concluded, had begun at birth. Do you remember the story of Victor? Loving, caring touches had no place in his life.

Yet touch is, for the most part, not approved of in our culture. Men especially are often fearful of being labeled homosexual or effeminate if they touch one another. Touch often is not a part of family life. It is too often absent as a basic communication between parents, infants, children—especially between fathers and children.

Many persons—in a touch-deprived culture such as ours—jump to false conclusions when touch does indeed occur. The strong feelings that can accompany much needed touch may send a person head-over-heels in love. Some persons who work with teenagers believe that the need for touch and the feeling of affirmation it conveys is what brings many teenagers to premarital sex, using the following progression:

TOUCH $\longrightarrow$ LOVE $\longrightarrow$ SEX

It is fairly easy to see the weakness of this kind of reasoning. Nonetheless each of us needs loving, caring touches regardless of our state of life—whether married, single, or religious. And we must realize that a caring touch or an embrace need not be a signal for sexual relations, nor even a loving relationship. For example, an embrace in some cultures may be just a sign of greeting.

Social Pressure and Acceptance

According to the **Newsweek** article mentioned previously, social pressure from dates, friends, and peer groups is a major reason for teenagers having sex: "Many teenagers are having sex as much because it is available and fashionable as because it is desirable." Not long ago, chastity was the social "norm," the value supported by most people. Today that norm is gone. The message we get now is that sex is "what's happening." So gaining social acceptance often means becoming involved in or lying about having sex:

> **Now an uncommonly virtuous teenager lies to protect the dirty little secret that she is still a virgin. There is more pressure than ever to "get it over with."**

Moreover, the cultural pressures on young men still compel them to actively seek premarital sexual relationships. As one nurse explains it: "What's to prevent a young man from exploiting or being exploited by a girl . . . when society has taught him that being male means showing strength, winning, conquering—even in sexual relationships? He lives in a setting where the double standard still exists."

Behind this peer pressure is the set of consumer values most of us have adopted as members of our culture. A doctor who heads a clinic for teenagers responded with the following remark when asked why teenagers have sex:

> **We have all been raised to have what we want now. It is a "give me" society and everyone is out for what they can get. Kids have to learn they can't have it all now. They need to hear, "No, don't do it—wait."**

What do you think of the following statement, along the same lines, voiced by a high school teacher?

> **What hurts kids sexually is that they grew up in an instant gratification society . . . since birth they are used to turning on a TV button and getting what they want right now . . .**

Is that teacher—or the doctor—being too negative? Does anyone in your life advise you to wait for sex or suggest that remaining a virgin is OK?

The Overwhelming Need for Closeness

The connection between sex and the need for intimacy is a matter of concern to many people who counsel teenagers. Economic pressures and the rapid pace of life we all face do not leave people with much time for family, friends, even themselves. Many of us are left hungry for intimacy. As one family counselor put it: "It's a real hunger, like a drug hook, driving persons from one person to another—sexually or otherwise—looking for intimacy."

People who are very lonely turn to sex as a means of acquiring and sealing a friendship. Again, the family counselor:

> It is lonely people of any age, who leap to sex. It feels good. And unconsciously in looking for intimacy this way, they believe "everything will be OK if I can be with him or her." But sex doesn't bring intimacy. They are going at it backwards: sex has to *follow* intimacy to help it grow . . .
>
> I remember one guy who came in here after he had had one

affair after another. He finally got so lonely he had to come in, for he was afraid he'd never be able to really give himself in commitment, that he'd never have the relationship he really wanted. Sex, he realized, had become just a genital thing . . .

Another day I had a young man in here, about eighteen, who was impotent. He was worried to death about what was wrong with his manhood. You see, he'd been having sexual relations since he was fourteen. His body now was trying to tell him that sexual relations—separated from intimacy—were hurting him.

Poor Self Image

The teenage years are a time for forming a sense of self. Earlier we discussed what that means, including our coming to understand our physical and emotional development. And earlier, we discussed the basic human need for love, a need which is sharpened during this period, both because of these terrific changes during adolescence and because teenagers suffer a lack of affirming touch in our culture. These stresses threaten one's self image. A counselor of college students talks about this particular problem:

A lot of us don't believe in ourselves. When we're young, especially, we need friendships, intimacy, to affirm our own belief in ourselves. Self image and the roles we're taught loom large in our lives. . . . Guys, especially, are taught to live without real friendships: "Don't reveal your feelings of fear, weakness; be on top, be winners, be strong, don't show emotion. . . ." And girls soon learn that we're supposed to be on call to men for everything; that it's a man's love that gives us our worth, that men need us to be happy. . . .

We don't learn to communicate past these roles. We're too busy projecting our own picture of what our date ought to be or what we need from him or her. . . .

So look what happens. A guy and a girl are out on a date. Both like each other, want a supportive relationship. Neither one has a real strong self image, neither one has thought through clearly what they demand from a relationship, what they believe is right or wrong about premarital sex.

Picture them coming home from a movie. He parks the car. She cares about him, but certainly hasn't made a commitment of herself for life. She's still getting to know him, wants him to like her. He likes her, wants her affection, support, and is strongly sexually aroused.

So as he becomes more intimate physically, she is thinking, "I don't want to hurt him, I don't want to say no, I don't want him not to understand, to stop liking . . . how can I say no?" And he's thinking, "She must want me to go on, to continue, or she'd say stop."

And they soon have intercourse. Yet they never did have any real communication about it. What was its meaning in their lives?

The Christian View of Sex

All of these motives for having sex stem from real human needs: for acceptance, for closeness, for self-esteem, for touching. And, as the comments of the various teenagers and counselors suggest, in our society we expect that sex will take care of these and any other needs we might have. Unfortunately, sex cannot do this, and this fact is precisely the focus of the Christian stance regarding sex.

Before we discuss the Christian view, however, something about its history needs to be said. As a two-thousand-year-old organization with millions of members past and present, the Church cannot claim to have spoken with the clarity of a single voice or with a totally consistent understanding of sex. Remnants of earlier, unhealthful, negative teachings about sex darken its basically positive viewpoint.

To understand this, we have to realize that in classical, Western anthropology, human beings were thought to have two parts, a higher and lower nature. The higher nature—our mind and will—was supposed to keep in check the "raging beast" of our lower nature, the body, with its feelings of "lust" and "concupiscence."

In this view, sexual activity was a threat to our rational, "better" self, and women were sources of temptation—and degraded as such. To have any sexual life, even in marriage, made someone less good than a virgin.

One holdover from this view is that today, although we know better, sexual feelings still are not openly discussed. Ingrained into our society is the feeling that sex is not necessarily a good part of our human nature.

At the Second Vatican Council, the Church set the record straight on human sexuality. It said that our sexual needs and desires are just as much a part of the goodness of being human as are our mind and spirit, and that we reach the heights of holiness in an intimate, committed sexual love.

This love is an eminently human one since it is directed from one person to another through an affection of the will. It involves the good of the whole person. Therefore, it can enrich the expression of the body and mind with unique dignity.

Sol Gordon, a leading sex educator, puts the same thought into somewhat different terms: "Sex is a good thing, and important. It looms very large and menacing in a life that is empty and frustrating. It is an exquisite part of a life that is developing, searching, and striving for harmony."

These sources speak a common message: sex cannot meet all our needs, make us **who we are**—male or female. On the contrary, **who we are** makes sex what it is in our lives—either good and healing and exciting or else sinful and hurting.

An analogy will help put this discussion into more concrete language:

Suppose three strangers are standing in front of a theater, each of them wanting to go to a movie. It is a kind of super-theater with ten different films showing at once. One or two films are excellent and exciting; others are depressing and not worth the price of admission. The first person standing in front of the theater cannot read, not even the information on the billboards outside the theater. But all the billboards have the usual bright colors and attractive faces. What are his chances of choosing a film he might like? The second person *can* read the billboards. What are the chances she will make a good selection? The third person has spent part of the morning reading newspaper and magazine reviews of each of the films at the theater. She knows who is in the films, who directed them, the basic story lines, and what reviewers thought of the films critically. What are her chances of seeing a great and exciting film compared with the other two persons?

Every analogy has its limits, but the point to this one is this: before we decide to get into sex, we must learn to know ourselves, the other person, and the situation we are getting into. Otherwise, there is a very good chance we are buying a ticket to a lousy film—to use the terms of the analogy. And in real life that means someone can get seriously hurt emotionally or get pregnant with an unwanted child or become cynical and closed to love. On the other hand, by bringing more of ourselves and more understanding of the other person to the experience of sex, we have a much better chance of creating a loving and lasting sexual encounter. This is why the Church's view of sex is in fact a very positive one: it asks each of us to seek out the best, the most intimate, and most enduring love we are capable of.

Following are some guidelines to explain just when sex belongs in a relationship:

SEX SHOULD COMMUNICATE LOVE

Sex, like other gestures and like speech itself, expresses something. It can express a gift of total self or just momentary feelings or something somewhere in between. Sex can be an action of our body, or an expression of our whole being. What it means or communicates depends on us.

Think back to the sexual encounter the college counselor described. As she saw it, sexual acts can raise questions that are never spoken, force both persons to hide their real feelings, and, instead of bringing them together, actually create a gulf between them.

For the communication to be honest, an act of physical love should express interior love. People have to know each other very deeply to be assured that sex is communicating each other's love. That means people need to grow together, spend time together, learn about each other's past and future plans. This can be a long and sometimes painful process—and sex is no shortcut. On the contrary, sex without communication can tie people together who eventually find out they do not like each other much.

SEX SHOULD BE APPROPRIATE

If a sexual relationship is to be a gift of our whole selves, not just our bodies or a few hours of our time, the question arises as to whether or not an adolescent can make such a gift. Teenagers by definition are searching to discover themselves, trying to find identities separate from parents, friends, and authorities. Until the major issues of the whole self involved in this search are settled, how can a gift of the whole self be made?

Many young adults, still exploring relationships, are wary of commitment. Can the young adult, then, honestly include sex in his or her relationships?

Both can have intimacy in some ways. There can be deep affection, good friendship, loyal and total feelings of caring. But if love is to last, there must be enough sense of self and enough honesty so that each can say, "I give myself to our relationship permanently and totally."

As one teacher put it: "Sex doesn't belong in teenage relationships. How can anyone give himself or herself to another person when he or she is still trying to figure out who he or she is?" Would you agree or disagree with that?

SEX SHOULD BE RESPONSIBLE

In today's consumer society, sex is often seen as separate from committed relationships—as part of a short-term friendship or as an expectation in casual dating. As Christians, however, love demands that we take responsibility for our actions. Couples have a grave moral responsibility to face up to their intentions regarding intercourse and its consequences.

We should expect sexual intercourse to have profound effects not only on the couple who experience a deep and powerful emotional bond, but also between those two persons and any unborn life they may procreate. **Just as we should not consciously hurt another by dishonest, unloving, or irresponsible sexual acts, we should not risk the procreation of new life for which we will not take responsibility in its care and nurture.**

Contraception does not provide a solution to the issue of pregnancy outside of marriage. Just on the level of behavior, many young people do not use contraceptives because they feel that even having such devices or pills signals a willingness or a decision to have genital sex. Many begin to play a dangerous "sex game" which might be called the Surprised Virgin. In this "game" if someone chooses to have intercourse, he or she pretends to be totally unprepared for it, and, as a result, in refusing to face honestly the risks involved, might become pregnant or might make someone else pregnant.

As gravely important as it is for teenagers to avoid pregnancy, using contraception does not make sex morally all right. The Christian view of sex is as much concerned with the individuals involved as it is with any new life which they may procreate. And only love and commitment between two people, as should be found in a marriage relationship, can make sex what it should be.

SEX SHOULD INCLUDE COMMITMENT

Commitment is a decision to give oneself to another, to take responsibility for a relationship, to try to make it grow and endure. When sex expresses this type of commitment, it can bond even more closely the love that is present.

Sex without commitment falls short of this. It says, "You can have my body, but you can't have me." We are leaving part of ourselves out.

Commitment in love relationships is a freeing thing. It frees people from playing games, from worrying about rejection. Commitment allows two persons in love to concentrate on their relationship. It helps them grow to discover each other's needs, what is good for "we," what pleases the other. Committed love leads to marriage.

Father Gregory Kenny puts it this way: "In talking about sexual relationships, the reference point should and must be marriage. . . . Once a couple decides it is moral to have a sexual relationship, they are making the decision to get married." Why? Father Kenny believes it is because "marriage is the public announcement of a mutual commitment that already exists." If the commitment exists, the announcement naturally follows.

All four of these moral guidelines—regarding communication, appropriateness, responsibility, and commitment—are challenges reflecting the Church's belief that sex is extremely good and important in our lives, that it is both a love-building and a life-giving act. And in recognizing the power and promise in sexual acts, the Church asks a question each of us must answer honestly and thoughtfully: "Why not the best?" We deserve nothing less.

SEX SHOULD BRING JOY, PLEASURE, SHOULD DEEPEN LOVE

When the sexual relationship of two persons means "we love each other, we give ourselves to each other, and we take responsibility for that commitment in our life together," their sexual love is freed from some built-in fears and restraints which in the long run will limit the pleasure and mutual joy of that love. They have freed themselves to grow in intimacy. This will be discussed further in the chapter on sex in marriage.

FOR REVIEW

1) What is the difference between sex and sexuality?

2) Describe what is meant by our society's double standard regarding sexual morality.

3) Explain the key differences between male and female sexual arousal.

4) Define infatuation and explain how it is different from sexual arousal.

5) List the various reasons teenagers and counselors give for teenagers having sex. Discuss each reason briefly.

6) Why can it be said that the Church's view of sex is basically a positive one?

7) Explain each of the six guidelines regarding sex and our relationships.

FOR REFLECTION

1) Make a list of your five favorite records. Next to each title:
   a) Indicate (yes/no) whether the song is primarily about sexual matters.
   b) Indicate on a scale of 1 to 10 how you rate the moral (10) or immoral (1) tone of the lyric.
   c) Explain briefly why you scored each song the way you did.

2) Write a poem about someone you care for. Do not worry about rhythm or rhyme. Try this method for creating a poem:

In a column write down three physical traits of the person (for example, sandy-haired, freckled, skinny). Then, list three character traits (for example, anxious, daring, witty). Then, list three roles (tennis player, friend, dancer). Now you have the makings for at least a three-line poem with three or four words in each line (for example, sandy-haired, daring tennis player/skinny, anxious dancer/freckled, witty friend . . .).

People in Their Lifestyles 6 Can Become Sacraments

How Do We Experience Our Lives as Sacraments?

The last chapter marked the end to our study of relationships in our past and present lives. This chapter marks the beginning of our examination of various "future" lifestyles and relationships—the single life, the lifestyles of priests and religious, married life, parenting, and family life. One or some of these will soon become a part of your future.

Among the many decisions we face regarding what lifestyle to choose is this one: "What role, if any, will Christian faith and the Church play in my life?" In this chapter, we will investigate how our lifestyles themselves can reflect our faith in God and our membership in the Church. And understanding how our lives can become sacraments is central to that investigation.

Often we learn to think of a sacrament as something fixed and defined, but not easily understood: "A sacrament is an outward sign of inward grace." Trying to add meaning to that definition, we might attach a list of the seven Catholic sacraments—Baptism, Eucharist, Penance, Confirmation, Holy Orders, Matrimony, the Anointing of the Sick. If we want to think of our own lives as sacraments, however, we need something more than a definition or a list. We need to be able to describe what happens when we experience a sacrament fully.

We can begin working up that description by looking first at the meaning that the seven sacraments have in people's lives. This is an

excellent place to start because one of the major purposes of the sacraments is to help **us** to become sacraments. So in reading through the following comments by various people, ask yourself these questions:

In what ways are their statements similar or different?

How do these persons' feelings about the sacraments agree with or differ from my own?

"Sacrament," responded a young personnel manager, single, age twenty-nine, "means a lot to me. It means first at Baptism, someone saying to us, 'You're chosen, you're blessed . . . life and love is in you . . . God loves you.' Then in Confirmation it says, 'You're choosing that life.' "

"Sacrament," responded one man, a father of six, "is one of the significant events that change a person's life. Look at what we do at a wedding. We show that something has *really happened* to that couple. The bride and groom are at the altar, surrounded by family and friends. They're holding a celebration: flowers, music, prayers, ceremony, food, excitement. It's a real sign that God's life comes through this event that's taken place."

"Sacrament?" said a religious, a teacher, age thirty-four. "It means I've got a responsibility to myself but to all the other people in my life too. Sacrament means not being judgmental about others, responding to them as best you can. We're reminded of this every day in celebrating the Eucharist: Look at God. He loves forever . . . we're all called to do that."

"What sacrament means to me," reflected a woman married twenty-two years, a mother of five, "is that there's something more than both of you in a marriage . . . a reason to stay other than the pleasure and support gained from each other. It's a sign to everyone of an unbreakable bond."

Not everyone experiences the sacraments in the forceful, positive way these people did. These comments are clear descriptions, however, of what the sacraments are intended to do. And when we experience them fully, the way these people did, our lives become (1) signs of

God's presence and love, and (2) signs revealing our choices regarding our futures.

1) **The sacraments are signs of God's love happening now in our lives.** As one writer puts it, they can be "God-charged" moments in which we sense that God is present, closer to us than at other times.

We are not always open to God's presence. Life is busy, complicated, and sometimes painful. For example, we may have to endure family hardship, the break-up of our parents' marriage, frustrations or failures at school or in our friendships. We can find ourselves surrounded in the world by people who are also suffering, and we are sometimes outraged by the evils that torment others.

Yet the sacraments point to the fact that all of life is "God-charged" and that, because God lives in history and since Jesus' Resurrection, there is more love and grace in the world than evil.

> **"It means first at Baptism, someone saying to us, 'You're chosen, you're blessed . . . life and love is in you . . . God loves you.' "**

> **"We show that something has *really happened* to that couple . . .**

> **"It's a real sign that God's life comes through this event."**

2) **The sacraments are signs of our choices regarding the future.** Each of the seven sacraments points to important events which shape our future. Baptism, for instance, is meant to signal our joining the Church. Confirmation is a sign of our mature and whole-hearted acceptance of that fact. And marriage is a sign of our acceptance of another person in deep and lasting love. The sacraments are meant to help us to look ahead in our lives, to make **conscious, heart-felt** decisions regarding our futures.

It is not often that we have clearcut answers to questions regarding our futures: How am I going to live and work? What contribution can I make? What values will I follow? Even when it comes to the most important decisions of our lives, regarding career, relationships, or lifestyles, most of us have a hard time looking ahead. Often we see the "turning points" of our lives only in retrospect:

"I married my wife because I wanted very badly to have someone to lean on, to share my shortcomings. I found out later that wasn't enough."

"I fell madly in love with my husband in a romantic sense, with all the tingles and all the bells. Our real commitment to each other didn't happen until a couple years later."

"It was only after I became a sister that I realized it meant more than just pursuing my own projects and priorities."

"We had a baby, we got married, we fell in love."

The sacraments help us look toward our future, asking us to make a commitment to it:

". . . in Confirmation it says, 'You're choosing that life.' "
"God loves forever . . . we're all called to do that."

How Do We Build Our Lives into Sacraments?

A traditional definition of sacrament was recalled earlier: "an outward sign of inward grace." Today the idea of sacrament has been expanded to reach into our individual lives. Now we speak of the call of **all** Christians to become sacraments in a sense, to make their own lives "outward signs" of the presence of God and of grace in the world.

To say that we are called to be signs of God's love, however, does not mean that we should become heroes overnight. It simply means that we decide to carry out, as best we can, Jesus' call to love God and neighbor. Furthermore, we should become aware that some lifestyles we might choose are more in line with his example than are others. Persons who are busily pursuing consumer relationships of all kinds— acquiring things, using people—are not likely to spend much time helping others or building close, lasting relationships. We can find opportunities to follow Jesus' example in any circumstance.

Our lives become sacraments as we recognize this fact. God's love happens only "now," in our own lives with others around us. Once we gain this insight, we can begin to see how people frequently act in kind and trustworthy ways—in hospitals, homes, offices, and factories. Instead of focusing on evil, for example, the airplane crash headlining the morning newspaper, we can, instead, reflect on the thousands of flights that arrive safely—on how many people must be doing their jobs conscientiously and skillfully to insure each successful flight. Our faith grows as we recognize life's goodness and our role in it.

Moreover, we become signs of God's love as we become more hopeful and thoughtful about our commitments. This faith and hope allow us to help shape the future. Through our careers, relationships, and commitments we can bring God's love to a world calling out for that love.

All Christians, then, share a common "vocation," to become sacraments in this sense. Our major choices in this process are important and should be celebrated. They also warrant asking for guidance from people we respect and our personal prayers for God's direction. As one writer puts it, to

"ask the Holy Spirit to make me a creature of love, a loving person in the human family and in the Church . . . "

In looking ahead to the person you want to become and to the lifestyle you might choose, it helps to consider the **particular** "sacramental" (or "sign") qualities people can achieve in the four traditional lifestyles.

SINGLE PERSONS

Until recently, neither our society nor the Church considered the single life as a genuine lifestyle. It was seen, instead, as a temporary stage of life for persons too young to make a commitment to marriage, to the religious life, or to the priesthood. In fact, for a long time only people who entered the priesthood or the religious life were said to have "vocations." It was only in the 1930s that marriage began to be considered a real vocation.

Today, we recognize that all Christians possess a vocation. The single life—temporary or permanent—is seen as a valuable commitment.

There are many different kinds of singleness—of young people and older people, widowed or divorced. The kind of singleness that will concern us here, however, is that of the young adult.

The young, single adult should not feel that he or she is just

marking time until "settling down" in marriage or some other form of permanent commitment. The particular "sign" quality of the single life lies in its comparative freedom to discover and to develop one's gifts, to search through various commitments, learning from the difficulties and mistakes. It also lies in its freedom to make a commitment to a career of service without the restrictions imposed by a family or a religious community. This searching or open kind of lifestyle can serve as an example to other people of the unfinished, visionary view Christians should have regarding the world. Every Christian should see himself or herself as a pilgrim or a traveler, journeying toward the future with great expectations.

PERSONS IN THE RELIGIOUS LIFE

The term "religious," as it is used here, simply means "living by a rule" (from the Latin **religare,** meaning "to bind"). Many different forms of religious life have been adopted through the ages, some more devoted to prayer, some to action. What they have in common is a commitment, permanent or temporary, to follow a rule of life designed to help people grow in the love of God and service of God and neighbor..

This commitment has included celibacy, or remaining unmarried—chosen for the freedom it should provide to follow the religious commitments and to provide a sign to other Christians of the reality of God's love, beyond and within human love. And, except for the rare vocation to a hermit's life, it includes commitment to a community of persons following the same rule and making their communal life a sign to others of the loving community of Christ.

The sign qualities of the religious life are valuable to the Church and to society. People in the religious life give up marriage, not their development as human beings. They demonstrate the fact that we can become "whole" persons without sexual intercourse. Moreover, religious communities today offer various, workable models of community, which can broaden our ideas of Christian living and expand our notions of "family."

MARRIED PERSONS

The sacramental quality of married life is suggested in the Bible. The Hebrew Scriptures speak frequently of the relationship between the Lord and his people in terms of a marriage. And St. Paul speaks of the "profound mystery" of marriage as related to Christ and the Church. At the point in history when these interpretations were first written, they upgraded both marriage and the status of women. For in those cultures, a woman was legally the property of her husband, and arranging a marriage was a matter of business rather than of love.

These abuses belong to the past. More recently, the women's movement has brought new meaning to St. Paul's words that "there is neither male nor female, for you are all one in Christ Jesus." Marriage should provide an example of nurturing love as a sign of God's love. All of us know couples who, in spite of difficulties, demonstrate that deep and lasting love is possible, and that sharing love and life itself is worth doing. Such families radiate great warmth and joy, and offer hopeful examples of commitment to intimacy and a belief in marriage and family life. They are needed by other families and individuals in their communities. And they need others as well because the family cannot survive without the support of and service to the wider community.

PERSONS AS PRIESTS AND DEACONS

Priests and deacons make up the group in the Church who choose, as a sign, to officially serve the other members of the Church. A phrase that is often used to describe priests is the "servants of the servants of God." Priests share with everyone else in the Church the common vocation to become more effective signs of God's love and grace. They live a commitment to make Christ's presence visible in all Christian lifestyles by leading in the celebration of the sacraments and by leading in the search for Jesus' spirit in our lives. The lifestyle of priests includes being celibate. Also, only men have been permitted to be priests. While Church authorities have decided that, because of priests' special commitments, these conditions are necessary, some people argue against these restrictions, seeing much meaning in Paul's insight, quoted above, that there is "neither male nor female" and questioning the necessity of clerical celibacy. Discussion and study regarding these conditions are ongoing.

Both single and married men can be deacons. The sign quality demonstrated in their role is clear from the term itself: deacon means "server." Those who are deacons, like the whole Church and all of its members, serve the human family united in Christ.

All of these lifestyles, it might be noted, are complementary to one another—and interdependent. To see this, let us look at examples of persons who live these lifestyles in the following chapters. And, finally, we will consider how people from all walks of life are connected—in Jesus' vision—in the "world family" today.

FOR REVIEW

1) Explain what all of the Church's sacraments are signs of.

2) In what two ways do we become sacraments?

3) Explain the special sacramental qualities of each of the following lifestyles: single, religious, married, priesthood.

FOR REFLECTION

1) Write a table of contents for a book about your life up to the present. List ten chapter titles: for example, "A Red-Headed Girl Is Born in Brooklyn" or "I Become a Boy Scout" and so on.

2) Rewrite the table of contents for your life to include the years up to the year 2010. Include no more than ten chapters.

3) Taking into consideration all that has been said so far regarding Christian faith, relationships, and lifestyles, write a brief letter of intent about the kind of person you will be ten years from now.

Choosing the Single Life 7

Remaining Single

Most of us begin our adult lives in a single lifestyle. Today, however, more people than ever before are living in a permanent or long-term state of being single persons. For some it is through circumstance; but for many it is by choice—so many that for the first time the United States Census Bureau tells us that the traditional family no longer constitutes the majority of American households.

Not long ago a teacher in a girls' high school asked one of her senior classes how many of them might choose to remain single. Three-fourths of the girls raised their hands. Five years earlier this would not have happened. Today growing numbers of young women are exploring new options as career people. More and more young men and women are taking a second look at their willingness to make a life commitment to another person "till death do us part." Growing numbers of divorced people find themselves alone when they least expected it. And as the life span increases, unprecedented numbers of elderly persons, most of them women, are outliving their spouses by several years.

"Being single" as a deliberately chosen lifestyle is showing up even in the media: we see TV shows about career women or single parents. We read newspaper and magazine articles which explore all the facets of living alone.

It is becoming increasingly important for every young adult to think through what is involved in being a happy single person. And there is a growing awareness that each of us—whether single, married, or priest or religious—needs to be our own person if we are to love another well. In terms of what is really important in life, each of us is a "single person." All that really separates us from one another is the lifestyle we choose, the commitments we make, the role and intensity of the relationships in our own lives.

Up to now this course has focused on relationships in general. This chapter explores what is important in the lives of several single persons. The next chapter deals with priests or religious persons—single persons with a special commitment. Neither chapter is meant to be a definitive collection of facts and figures about the single or religious lifestyle. Instead, each tries to explore something more basic than that—asking real people what specific things are important to them for a fulfilling life.

The persons in both chapters were not chosen because their lives are representative of all the attitudes and situations that single or religious persons have or should have. But each one does have something unique to say that gives us insight into our own lives and relationships. Each is different from the others, yet, as you read, many similarities run through their reflections. Each of them is or wants to be involved with life. Each is at peace with who he or she is. Each one is a caring, nurturing person.

They are not there to be judged. Instead, we should use them as starting points to begin our own questioning of others we know, searching out the things that remain the important human constants of our changing lives.

As we read, two following points should stand out:

1) No person lives out his or her life as some fixed, unchanging thing—if he or she is alive and responding to life. Each of these people in this and the following chapter has undergone changes in his or her life.

2) Each one of us, regardless of the lifestyle we choose, has the same human and spiritual needs: we each need to love our own self, to grow in life and love, to love and be loved by others, to be close to others, to have some kind of community, to have meaning and some kind of permanence in our lives.

As you read this chapter, try to discover how each person expressed these needs in his or her unique way. Read to discover the roles that people and change have played in their lives. Try to see their words and lives not as a closed book but as the chapter where they happen to be right now. With that same feeling of openness to life, ask yourself the following list of questions as you read, keeping in mind that reading is an introduction, not a finished statement, of your own exploration of what is involved in being a single person.

Questions about aspects of our lives that carry us through change:

1) Does he/she like himself/herself? Is he/she growing as a person?
2) What place does friendship have in his/her life? How is his/her sexuality related to friendship?
3) What place does intimacy have in his/her life? What place does service have in his/her life? Is there a successful balance between commitments to service and intimacy?
4) Is he/she lonely? Why? Why not?
5) What does his/her happiness and fulfillment come from? What part do others play in this? Does he/she love others?
6) On what is his/her life centered? What gives his/her life direction?
7) How does he/she respond to change? Do relationships with others play a part in this?

Interview: Bob Ryan

Bob, now age thirty-one, taught high school until a year ago. Currently he works in a large inner-city business concern.

If we're going to talk about lifestyles and look for guidelines about how to live with other people, I think we should look first at what's happening to people all around us. This is where revelation is, God's presence speaking to us in the lives of people we know. . . .

Two nights ago I was in the store near my apartment and this guy came in, very sharply dressed, big car, the whole works. He set down his stuff at the counter—it was pop, potato chips, cold cuts—and he got real angry at the counterman. I could just see the pain in this guy's eyes, so when I got in line behind him I said to him, "You're divorced, aren't you?"

He looked at me and said, "What's it to you?"

"Nothing," I said, "I just noticed it. I think you're divorced."

"No," he said, "but we're in the process. I've been out of the house now for about a month. How did you know?"

"Look at what your order is! People who've been single for a long time don't live on Fritos and cold cuts."

"Yes," he said, "but I don't know how to deal with it . . . my career . . . "

"I know," I said. "I can tell just by the way you're talking with the guy at the check-out counter . . . you're used to being the boss, you know. But is your career making you happy?"

"No," he said. "Can't you tell?"

Well, I just can't get the guy out of my head—the pain he's in, the divorce. That "masculine" thing—it's the only thing that's giving him support in his life right now, except it's also the very thing that's undermining him. So I'm just thinking that I'd look to that man to give me some answers about lifestyles. That's revelation speaking to us.

The other thing that's really important is that we have to love ourselves. I've got to love myself and that love has got to grow and spread to others. The minute it starts to sit just in me it starts to shrink, die. It's like yeast: to keep yeast alive it's got to grow; otherwise it starts dying and gets smaller. Any lifestyle ultimately is the way we express our love . . . whether we're married, single, or religious.

So anytime you talk about lifestyles I only ask about one thing: Is it life-giving? Will it support and enable that person to be life-giving?

I live alone except for a friend, Jack, who moves in and out. But I'm not lonely. If I do stay single, it wouldn't be choosing to be alone because single life to me is still a choice to share love with people on an ongoing basis—with a talent or in a special position or to a group of friends committed to something you believe in . . .

Sometimes people say "Are you single? That's too bad, you'll have to get married." But I'm sitting there thinking, "Now wait a minute, marriage isn't going to take care of loneliness or make life worthwhile. It's going to be an expression of however I find my life." If you're giving love, giving life, a person doesn't have to be a religious or married to be happy . . .

And not only that: I'm ministering to people . . . to friends, in the job, in community involvement. At first I thought I was going to get married *period* because not to get married would mean I'm selfish—but this life isn't so selfish . . .

Yet I want a committed love relationship, and I'm still working on that. I make decisions in line with that. Even my job, my use of time, things—all take second place to that. I still want that because it's the only way I think I could grow.

What's "life-giving"? Well, supposing your goal is to make a million. Look at the poverty level! I could judge that every millionaire causes four poor families. That's not very life-giving, is it? Supposing my life project were to master wood carving. Is wood carving a cause of other people's suffering or poverty? It's not the same, is it?

This might sound simple to you but life is really good to me—so good that I feel guilty about it. Just the other night as I walked out of the post office and the sky was so beautiful, I felt so happy . . . I know, there are so many lonely people! (Not that I'm never lonely.) But no matter what I'm doing I enjoy people. If I were to be unemployed tomorrow, I just know that I'd find myself enjoying talking to the guy in front of me. My stability is that I enjoy people. And my worth, I guess, comes from the fact that I'm a child of God—not from what I own, or what I do or don't do. Life is really good to me.

Interview: Ann Zanzig

Ann is a single, thirty-three-year-old assistant dean of students at a university in West Virginia. Ann is responsible for housing and many student programs outside of the classroom. The university has a student population of about twelve thousand, about two thousand of whom live on campus.

I guess I never made a conscious decision to go into counseling as a career. I would say that a lot of it had to do with coming from a large family. I think you acquire some traits and personal characteristics that are good for counseling—tolerance, exposure to different lifestyles, that kind of thing. You learn to be a listener, and I think that's probably the greatest quality that a counselor utilizes. I found through my friends and family that counseling was something that seemingly I was good at, and so I stuck with it. I thought I had something to offer the profession and vice versa.

I have been happy with the decision. I waver at times, of course. If I were to leave the field, I would miss, in particular, the energy and good feelings generated from being around students.

In regard to how my career fits into my life, I think it takes up a greater portion of my time as a single person than it would for someone who is married. I would say that a good 80 percent of what I do is job-related. I think that's one of the myths about the single lifestyle . . . that it must be nice because you can go home and don't have the family there; you don't have "responsibilities." But if you are a single person in a career, particularly a career where you are with people a lot or people look to you for leadership, people tend to think that you are never off duty. Consequently, you can many times be much more taken up by projects and by people than if you aren't single.

I have often said that not one day goes by that I don't learn something in my career, and I think that is probably one of the things that make it fulfilling and make me continue with it.

Much of the morning is in administrative work—staff meetings, long-range planning, dealing with budgets, responding to memos—of which there are thousands. Most of the rest of the day is spent in meetings with student groups—helping freshmen students, an alcohol education program, dorm government, the college bowl team. . . . In between, I have lots of student "drop-ins" with every problem you can possibly imagine—academic, personal, friends having problems. And most evenings I do programming: I may be invited by a student organization to do something on human sexuality, values clarification, or time management.

If the people I spend time with are *not* connected with the university, I have probably met them through someone at the university. And in a situation like this—where the university is at the center of the community—it is difficult to find someone who doesn't have some connection with it.

I think it's very, very important for someone in a single situation to know him- or herself very well and to like themselves—and I guess overall just generally to feel good about themselves. And to do that you have to spend some time with yourself. So I would say that my top commitment is to myself—to make sure that I always remember to make time for myself. The next commitment would have to be to serving students and hoping that something we do for them is going to improve their lives in a positive way. What gives my life direction is really others. Which is not to say that I don't have my own mind and my own goals and objectives, but rather that I really like to see what people's needs are and to try to respond to them . . .

Regarding sexuality, I don't think there is any situation, particularly as a female in a career, in which sexuality is lost in the shuffle. In dealing with students or colleagues—whomever you're dealing with—sexuality is never *not* there. When I deal with people, when I react to people, I am number one a female. That is always there. I think what I have been able to do somewhere along the line is clarify my own personal values . . .

I think that sex is beautiful and important whether it is physical or whether it is sexuality in terms of just males and females in all kinds of friendships. I think that if someone wants to enter into a sexual relationship, wants to have intercourse, there has to be something beyond just that act. Those are decisions that people, particularly young people, have to learn to face. What am I willing to commit to another person? How serious do I want the relationship to be? What is my responsibility to myself and to that other individual? And those are decisions that you have to make for yourself; I don't think there's any magic formula that I'd suggest to anybody. Personally I feel good enough about myself that I don't feel I have to use sex in order to gain respect or in order to gain attention.

I have thought about marrying a lot. I don't think it's fair to say that there is such a thing as a "marrying kind." I like to think I'm a kind of open book, and I'll see where my life takes me, and if that happens to be one of the things that happens to me, that will be fine. If not, I won't feel as if there has been a void. If I met someone whom I feli in love with and we wanted to marry, I would have to make some decisions in regard to my career, but I don't think that career and marriage have to exclude each other.

Nor have I made a decision that if I got married I would never have children or anything of that sort. I just have to say frankly that, if I didn't ever have children, I don't think I would feel as if I hadn't had a fulfilled life.

About being alone, again that's something people tell single people: well, let's see, you live alone, you must be lonely. That's not true. I think young people are often faced with the question of loneliness—in college and in high school, too. Again I would take it all back to how you feel about yourself. It's a big step if you have learned to be able to say to another person, "I'm feeling lonely today." And I could be with a group of people, I could be at a football game, I could be by myself, and I could have exactly the same feelings. Loneliness is not an unusual feeling, it's not something you alone are going through. And it is also something that you probably will have at certain times to certain degrees for the rest of your life. I don't attribute loneliness any more to my lifestyle than I would to any other lifestyle.

I might be in a unique situation: I'm not making a lot of money, but at least I do have a job. I think that the single person who is struggling with what career to choose or just not having a job would be in a different situation than I am in. And that's what a lot of young people are experiencing.

My happiness comes from being the person I am, and all that that includes. I don't think there's any one thing that makes me feel fulfilled. It is a combination of all the people that enter into my life every day—the good kinds, the bad kinds, people who are open to me and accepting and also the people who reject me. I think career and friends and family, all of that, are the things that fulfill me.

FOR REVIEW AND REFLECTION

Using the questions provided in this chapter, write a reaction to each of the two interviews presented.

Choosing to Be a Priest or a Religious 8

Space does not allow us to describe the varieties of lifestyle lived by priests or religious today. Nor can we give much more discussion of what is unique about the priest's or religious' special way of seeking and service to others than what we offered in chapter 6.

The varieties and uniqueness of lifestyle can probably best be found by reading and discussing them with men and women in the priesthood or the religious life today.

Nonetheless, the words of the priest and the religious persons you will read next are a very personal introduction to the religious lifestyle. They do not represent all the experiences and attitudes that all priests or religious have or should have. But they do convey the feeling that "religious are people too"—warm, sensitive, caring people who are working out their own lives and happiness in a special way.

As you read, it is important to remember that dramatic changes in the Church brought about by the Second Vatican Council affected the lives of priests and religious. Young men and women entering the religious life today will have a very different history from those who have been in religious life ten years or even five.

Yet if you were to be any one of those persons, great changes lie **ahead** for you also. As new issues confront the world, the Church will again respond to the various needs of people throughout the world. No one knows what lies ahead, but those interviewed suggest what some of the changes might be.

Back in an earlier part of the course, the Christian view of love was discussed as having incredible range. Jesus pursued commitments to service by nurturing people all around him—regardless of the fact that many of them were ignored or despised by society.

In the last chapter, the single people interviewed each felt that much of his or her life's meaning resulted from helping others. In this chapter, the people interviewed have formally dedicated their lives to helping others, to follow the example of Jesus. This commitment to serve others and to serve with others in community is a changing and growing process which can lead to unique and beautiful lives.

Read these interviews using the same list of questions you used in the last chapter, but add the following question to that list:

What is different about his/her life because he or she is a priest or religious?

Interview: Father Jack Olson

Father Olson, age twenty-eight, is an associate pastor in his second year in a suburban metropolitan parish of 1300 families.

Twenty-eight may seem young to you, but to me it seems like I've been a priest a lot longer than two and a half years. I first thought about the priesthood in second or third grade. I remember a sister helping me make a decision in fourth grade that it would be a good way to spend my life; I remember being excited by John XXIII at the age of nine. And at fourteen I went away to the seminary, but left it after high school graduation.

Then I pursued different service kinds of things . . . a continual search to help others. Finally after college I entered the seminary again. But it was still a year and a half before I was convinced I had a vocation.

When I think back on the priests in that small town I grew up in, I'm not really sure what first attracted me. I always admired them—the three we had. There was something attractive about them. They associated a lot with the adults and us kids. They tried to make us feel good, appreciated, see worthwhileness in our lives. They were warm, friendly, strong, leaders, special people, servants . . . not aloof . . . apart but touching others. They were good people, and happy. And Sunday Mass was important!

But as I got closer to ordination, what was I choosing? Well, it was maybe two things: one was this call to service . . . to be a priest who would be a leader or enabler of others. The other was a kind of lifestyle—that I could be a happy celibate person. And I knew that, unless I thought I could also be a good father and husband, I couldn't be a good priest either. It was only in the theologate that I was finally ready to say "yes," as much as anyone can.

A typical day as a priest is like this: up to celebrate Mass first thing, then time in the office with other staff on projects and phoning, maybe a luncheon meeting on a project or, often, just to get together with other priests or religious to share our lives and support each other. Afternoons might be an appointment, maybe an annulment, premarriage counseling, and then visiting someone sick or in a rest home; then maybe evening committee meetings. But I spend the largest share of my time on liturgy—that's my special area of responsibility on the staff.

The eight of us on our staff divide up the different areas of our parish work but we all share the counseling. My special area is liturgy and music.

Some days are twelve to fourteen hours but I make sure I limit myself to fifty to fifty-five hours a week. After that I'm not very effective. I learned—after putting in seventy hours a week—that unless I'm healthy and in touch and happy with who I am and what I'm doing, my ministry will be minimal. So I began to take time for myself.

So two days a month I use for that—for photography, museums, friends, reading, or maybe for a little more praying than I had found time for. And at nights I go home and relax.

But of all the things I do, the most rewarding—when you ask about it—is celebrating the Eucharist. To gather with people joined in faith and to celebrate that Sacrament is in a sense the greatest sign of who we are. I'm not the greatest innovator in the world, but I have a lot to share in homilies. And I pray well at

Mass. From the people at Mass I sense it's something important and meaningful to them—my praying with them, leading, being with them, and the sharing that goes with it . . . it helps us to get through the week and to learn more about who we are.

Another reward is the team concept on our staff—our sharing of ministry, our support of one another. Together we're all trying to help the whole community grow. We all share concern but then make our own full decisions.

You know, these aren't what I expected to be the best parts of the priesthood. When I was studying, I thought more along the lines of social justice. Those values aren't lost to me now; they're just exercised in different ways—through my preaching and homilies, writing in the bulletin, with the school kids . . . I learned that the parish is where the people are, where the action is.

Four of our staff sisters express these social concerns in the very simple lifestyles they've chosen. Our pastor also does this here in the rectory. He drives a used VW, buys very little clothing, gives a lot of his money to the parish, the poor, and others—but very quietly. I'm the one who has the hardest problem with that . . .

Maybe the hardest thing of all is to fail at times and live with that . . . to find out you were really screwing things up when you thought you were really doing something well. But there's also a liberation in that, when I realize that's part of who I am, of what makes me special as a priest. It's still hard, but it's liberating. And it's a disappointment, a disillusionment, when I can't meet an expectation someone has of the priesthood, or the Church, especially when it's a result of an earlier experience of that person.

Celibacy for me has been a very rewarding and satisfying lifestyle. In some ways it's freeing of my time and of my relationships, too. I treasure many friendships with priests, women and men religious, and lay people. If I had a family, I know a lot of my time would be directed toward the family members. I wouldn't have as many or as rich a kind of friendships as I have now because I am able to spend a lot of my free time with those people. I have relationships that I'm convinced are as deep and intimate in a psychological and emotional sense as many husband and wife relationships are.

As time passes I see a continual evolving of myself, too, a growing in confidence, in sharing of myself . . . now more through the ministry instead of just through my friendships as before.

And there's stability for me from three sources: the liturgy, my friends, and my family. They've always been there supporting me in who I am.

Am I lonely? No. You know, I live alone in an apartment because my pastor wanted me to have my own space, and I quickly came to appreciate that . . . I relax, unwind, and entertain if I want to. I cook, clean, do my laundry. Like the people I serve, no one waits on me. I don't find it lonely, I find it liberating . . . I'm more able to be who I am. I have people over and go out to others' places . . . it's not lonely at all.

The future? It may bring some changes in the Church. Our culture isn't really a Christian one . . . and we're going to have to give more and more support and help to people to live Christian lifestyles. I see our culture shirking its duty of ministry to the poor. Somehow, the Church is going to have to pick up some of that social ministry. And it's fun, in my imaginings of the future, to choose the ways my priesthood might respond to that some day.

Interview: Brother Thomas Sullivan, FSC

Brother Tom, age thirty-six, is currently director of a Christian Brother Candidate Program and has taught at the junior and senior high school levels in science and biology.

My family moved around a lot when I was young. I went to thirteen different grade schools and two high schools. Half of them were public, half were private, parochial. I attended a Holy Cross Brothers High School in Massachusetts. I already knew I wanted to teach, but there was something about the brothers at the high school that impressed me. Their esprit de corps, their dedication, their living together; they seemed to enjoy one another's company and worked together well. And they were good teachers.

My freshman year in college I met a girl from California, and the idea of becoming a brother went out the window for a couple years. But the question of what was I going to do after college came up again—approaching junior year—and I decided that maybe I should give religious life a try as long as the thought was still there in the background, much as I tried to push it away.

Once I joined the brothers, there were still choices to be made. I wanted to teach. So after I earned my education credits, I taught for two years in Oshkosh and seven years in Fridley, a suburb of Minneapolis. I had been asked previously to take over the candidate program, but did not feel I was ready for it. I was in the midst of developing some programs in ecology. The day of assigning people in our order without consultation with the individual is a thing of the past. But support, yes—not only from the local community but from the district, provincial staff, and other brothers as well. I talked to many brothers and close friends seeking their advice. I also spent a lot of time praying about the decision. Finally I decided to quit teaching and enter formation work. Now the decision I have to make is whether or not to go on to graduate school for my doctorate in biology.

There are a lot of opportunities and support for brothers. I feel, the way religious life is today, there is more drawing upon the talents of an individual and developing those talents rather than filling slots with people.

In the religious life, your relationship with God is basic, above the other things. I have had a couple close calls in life, situations in which I could have been snuffed out just like that. You begin to ask questions like: Why am I still alive? What's the purpose of life? Why was I created? I have talents; they've been given to me as gifts by God. How do I best use them in the world?

I feel that my life as a religious and as a teacher is challenging, and I guess that along with challenge and growth comes happiness which I feel is very important to a person's life. I guess if I weren't happy or if I felt that my life were not being fulfilled or if I felt I had reached a point where I were not growing, then I would think seriously that maybe this life was not for me.

I think that's an advantage of being a religious. You spend time reflecting on your life and making sense of your daily experiences in daily personal prayer, in community prayer, at retreats. We do a lot of reflecting, and not just navel-gazing because that can get very out of perspective. I look back on my life, and I feel I'm a better person now than I was last year and the year before that. I must be doing the right thing for me. It doesn't mean that I haven't had some rough periods in my life. I have! But I look back from year to year and I feel I'm growing, I think there is a lot of my potential still to be tapped.

You have to be able to deal with loneliness and aloneness, yet it's important to know there are supportive people around you. The times when I feel lonely are times when I can't communicate with people or when I find it frustrating dealing with a best friend. As far as feeling depressed, however, those times are few and far between.

Regarding sexuality, I am only speaking from my own experience. I wouldn't want to speak for all religious because I think every person has their own life experiences. But for myself my decision to become a religious, to take the vow of celibacy, was a challenge. Everyone is a sexual person. And there's the whole masculinity thing. I know in talking to young men about the brothers that it's the celibacy aspect that stops a lot of them. They are interested in God, community, and service, but celibacy seems to be the stumbling block. They don't know if they can live it. And all I can say is: that's right, maybe you can't. I don't think it is for everybody. However, I don't think marriage is for everybody either. I think the high divorce rate points this out.

I've always been very comfortable with both men and women. I don't feel that my sexuality is lessened because I show "feminine" characteristics like love, tenderness, compassion. We're all male and female: there are both dimensions in all of us.

Intimacy is an important part of my life. It is expressed in many ways other than genitally. I need people with whom I am intimate, close to—which to me means being completely open and free with. That's important to me. It helps keep my life and person in perspective.

My brother and his wife are Mormons with eight children. My

sister-in-law, Kathy, has a very difficult time understanding my celibate lifestyle because, in their religion, their whole life is family-oriented. It really amazes her that I love children as much as I do. She says, "I can't understand it. You ought to be married. You'd make a good father. You ought to have kids." That's a compliment. I think that if I didn't like kids I shouldn't be a brother either. Because then I would think that my life as brother might be an escape; it would no longer be a choice. There *are* days, however, when I think about the fact that my choice means I will never have any children.

That's where community comes in. Getting to know the brothers, interacting with them, living with them, praying with them, recreating with them. All of this provides a supportive group of men with whom I share myself and my life. And our communities change frequently. I am constantly meeting new people—new brothers. People I'm not living with now may move into my life on a much more intimate basis later as I live with them or join their community.

I feel there is a balance between my personal needs and my life work—mainly because I take time to maintain it. A lot of brothers are becoming re-educated in this whole area of work vs. personal needs and of dealing with their feelings, their emotions, their sexuality. As a result, more brothers are seeing a need for balance—which in some lives is not there.

It's very American—the Protestant work ethic. We are not useful unless we are productive. It's also an occupational hazard of the religious because of our commitment to service. Some become so service-oriented that they neglect their personal lives. And once that happens and they drift away from the people they live with, they drift away from the brothers.

I'm a busy person—taking classes, teaching, meetings, formation work—and it often gets hectic. There are times when I just have to say no. But I'm a happier person for it. I also need people close to me to say, "Tom, you're overdoing it." And I'm lucky enough to have those people.

I think the role of the religious is changing a lot. Basically it's still associated first of all with the Church, which is also in flux. But where I see the role of the religious today—and it becomes clearer to me the longer I'm a religious—is that the brother is free to take a stand without intimidation. He must become a prophet and a pilgrim. To be a prophet today means one must be committed to justice and human rights. We must *live* our words rather than merely speak them. When something is going on at school, for instance, and a faculty member feels very strongly about it, he or she often can't challenge it because, if he or she does, it may mean the loss of a job. On the other hand, I have less to lose if I speak out and, as a result, they "can" me tomorrow. I have a supporting community behind me. With its finances, with its geographic reach, I can most likely find other work and people who need help.

And I think the stronger the community support for its members, the more religious are going to be able to take those risks. Worldwide, in the third world countries especially, there are real social justice issues at stake. Then there are also the issues of minorities, homosexuality, sexism, the whole gamut. They are not popular issues on which to take a prophetic stand.

Life for me as a religious is centered on my God relationship, a response to his call. Prayer and meditation help me to focus on the relationship. But beyond that come community and service. I couldn't be a hermit. There are differences in religious life, and the type of religious life which I choose is the active, apostolic rather than the more contemplative. I believe in the power of prayer, and I believe that there's a lot of good to be done through prayer. But I feel that I have to be more active. I feel that is God's special calling for me.

Interview: Sister Frances Edwards

Sister Frances, fifty years old, has been a staff person for three years on a diocesan program.

I've been a sister in my order for over thirty years. I entered at eighteen and was either a teacher or principal in a school for twenty-five years. In that time, many changes have come about in the Church and in my life.

I think we were really getting to who we are. And I think we've come to separate what we do from who we are. Now I talk to a lot of young people and many are amazed to find that sisters do so many things besides teaching and nursing.

I also gradually began to take a serious look at vows—not that they were ever a light thing to me—but at how my life now was different. I had an unmarried brother teaching too and our lives seemed parallel. "Gee," I thought, "my life ought to be different from his!"

He's a layman, I'm vowed. He was in about the same situation I was in. Not much money, he wasn't going to have sexual relationships with anybody. But he could go away every weekend and do his thing—travelling, outdoor things. I thought, "There's a difference," and the meaning of obedience began to come to me. That's really important!

So at various times during these years each vow would assume an importance. At one time it might be celibacy, at another, poverty. I guess what I'm saying is that instead of going just day after day, getting up in the morning and living out your life, I was having to and wanting to take a look at what those vows really mean for me. It might sound strange, that I could live all of those years, following routines, not being that aware. Now I dressed like all the lay teachers and I wasn't one. So my senses were bringing me to the fact that I'm not a layperson. Should it make a difference? And communities went through all those things too.

We began asking, "Were we better than?" But you know, there is no "better than," strictly speaking. So then we went through, "we're not better but we're the same as." Well, that didn't sit well with me because we weren't the same as. A married lay person has a whole different way of living! We're still in some of that line of thinking: should a way of life, should what you do and what I do all be the same?

Well, when you ask me what is different, obedience certainly was different. I wasn't footloose and fancy-free. I belonged to this community; it's a responsibility thing. But even that's changed. And I really did a lot of thinking about this, especially when I made the decision to leave teaching.

I heard about this job and I went to my superior, my pastor, and my local community where I lived. They all encouraged me to pray and look into it. And when I got the job, I went to them for final permission.

If the superior had, at any time, said, "No, don't go any further, this community needs you in a different way," I wouldn't have pursued it. But the big difference was that fifteen years ago I would never have initiated any change or new program for myself. Applications for jobs went to the superiors and they called you in to say "Want to look at this?" or "I want you to take this job." There was little consultation of my feelings, my hopes—nobody ever asked me if I wanted to go into teaching!

Now you initiate! A superior can say no, but she wouldn't do it lightly, and when she does, we know she has the overview of the whole community in mind. I don't know of any community today where a provincial is going to say, "Do this," the way it used to be.

So what is it essentially being a sister? Well, for me, serving as a member of *this* family is part of it; but if being a sister, working priest, brother isn't saying that I, Frances Edwards, vow my life to God, he is the center of my life, if that's not the *first* thing, I say, then I don't think I'm a sister. I could be a teacher, an administrator, in this big office, but if God isn't first in my life, if prayer isn't the essential of my life, if community isn't an essential in my life, I've got it all wrong. Why encumber myself with a lot of extra stuff if it's meaningless?

So I guess I really throw myself to God on the flow of life. These things are slow to happen. But that's the movement religious life is in now, an emphasis on consecrated life. It doesn't matter what I do as a person—and that's becoming true in most communities. And in the future it won't be a surprise to me if we won't have Benedictines, Dominicans, Sisters of St. Joseph— that we become more daughters of the Church, so to speak. I can see that possibility, even now. Already sisters of different orders work together on things, and in some cases live together.

And this gives sisters flexibility, this emphasis on conse-crated life. I see here right in this city—in my own community— things that ten years ago you wouldn't have heard of: centers, homes for people with problems. We didn't even talk about battered women. Now here we are, serving them. We even have some sisters visiting in prisons.

So the needs I think are what speaks to where we go. When I think of the future, I don't know what the results are going to be—but events in South America, for instance, could open up another whole area for us.

FOR REVIEW AND REFLECTION

Using the questions provided in this and the previous chapter, write a reaction to each of the three interviews presented.

Choosing Marriage 9

Marrying Today

"Up to now, I've always thought of marriage as something for other people," said a high school senior shortly before her graduation this year. "It wasn't even real to me. But now I know people who are getting married or talking about marriage."

Perhaps you have gotten an invitation to the wedding of someone who graduated a year or two ago, or you have a friend who has talked of marriage. In one way or another, the topic will soon become a reality to you—something that affects the lives of people important to you, and your own life as well.

And well it should, for statistics show that most people marry. Nearly 95 percent of all Americans marry; only 6 percent of men and 4 percent of women remain unmarried throughout their lifetime. We are a very marrying society!

And for good reason. The love that is the core of a good marriage is something most persons hope to find in life. A good marriage is an accepting, caring relationship where a man or woman can be loved for the person he or she really is. It is a way to live a shared, meaningful life in trust, friendship, and honesty. As human beings we need these things in our lives and we search for them in our relationships.

Many marriages fall far short of this. Latest statistics suggest that nearly four out of ten new marriages will fail, leading some people to

predict that marriage is on the way out as a traditional way of life. But other experts say the opposite is true: that most people who divorce also remarry, seeking the long-term intimacy which lies at the heart of a good marriage.

What Do You Expect in Your Marriage?

If you were to marry tomorrow, what would your expectations be for marriage? What would you expect to get and give? Why would you have chosen the particular person you did?

A large city newspaper asked its readers to write letters describing the perfect mate. The wide range of responses showed how differently people view marriage.

One woman wrote that her husband most of all "makes me laugh" and she still loved him for that. Another noted how good it was that the man she had found was handsome. Others mentioned looks, too: "tall, dark, handsome" men, "blond, graceful" women, a "Robert Redford body," and a "Goldie Hawn" type were all listed as desirable qualities.

But most writers mentioned personal qualities, ranging from "inner beauty," "comfortable," "someone you can talk to," "sensitivity to my feelings," "intelligent, mind of her own,"—to someone to "fulfill all my needs and desires," "be dependent on me," "need me." Some were looking for an image, some for a sexual relationship, some for a person whose existence would center around themselves. Some were looking for a friend. What they wrote revealed a lot about their expectations and capacities for love.

If you were to list the qualities of a perfect mate, what would they be? Could you rank those qualities in order of importance? What would you list first? a certain image? looks? lifestyle? a successful person? certain social standing or accomplishments? Would it be the values, attitudes, or priorities of that person?

Would it be a list of qualities relating to how that person made you feel? Someone to make you feel strong, intelligent, confident, or happy? Would it be a list of qualities describing a good friend—someone to share your ideas and feelings, someone to enjoy doing things with? Would it be someone to have a good sexual relationship with, someone warm, affectionate, expressive?

Try to understand what you are looking for in love because your ideas about the ideal marriage and the ideal spouse reveal a lot about your capacity to love. Is your ideal lover someone who mostly gives to you? Or is he or she someone whom you would love to give to, whose happiness you could delight in?

Looking for the Right Lover

Have you ever had a friend who liked you because you had a car, or a lake cabin? Have you ever known a married couple who fell into certain roles, making each other feel strong or smart or successful—and when one person changed that a little, the whole relationship broke up? Did you ever have a friend who was unhappy when something very good happened to you: you might have lost weight or outshone everyone in a test or gotten an exciting gift—and that friend was more jealous than happy for you?

All of these relationships involved a dependency, a "receiving" type of love. There is never enough love for this kind of lover, psychologist Erich Fromm once wrote. He or she is like a "hoarder . . . anxiously worried about losing something." A good marriage requires giving people who are secure enough to see their spouse in an admiring, not a dependent, kind of love. Have you ever had a friend who could be so happy at something very good happening to you that you just knew he or she never thought of envy? Have you noticed how sometimes a parent delights in making a child happy without thoughts of what that child did for the parent in return? Have you ever known a middle-aged man, facing a dead-end in his own career, able to delight in his wife's beginning education or work? A good marriage grows through generous, "giving" love.

Think again of the most important qualities you would seek in a mate. Do you look at love as mostly a giving or a receiving relationship? Because of the times we live in, questions about giving and nurturing are the essential questions confronting anyone marrying today.

Some people say that, from our first flick of the TV button, we learned to expect and pursue quick pleasure. How do you react to the suggestion that media, advertising, lifestyles, our economic goals—our culture—have taught all of us that life is to be richly spent and fully enjoyed first of all for ourselves? Has an era of great consumption, cheap energy, quick and easy access to goods and entertainment conditioned us to pursue and enjoy these things as a kind of birthright?

Today, we bring many of these cultural expectations to marriage. Along with material desires we bring great personal needs, for it is also an era of many broken relationships and deep hurts.

Recently problems of energy and environment have cut into our consuming lifestyle. Fewer things and people, it seems, can be depended on to bring us what we have learned makes up happiness.

So, many people marry today fearing that "the good life" is disappearing. Further, for the first time in history, you can marry and contract against giving away too much. You can spell out what work you will do, how much you will share in finances, in child care, in career, in the home. Leading magazines feature marriage contracts that spell it all out. Love, many people think, is much too risky to give unconditionally.

Yet human needs have not changed. Despite the expectations of today, we still possess the same needs for loving, lasting relationships that our parents and grandparents had. An insecure world and new expectations have not replaced old needs for love, for intimacy that lasts. Instead, it is causing us to place even greater demands on marriage and relationships. So marrying today poses a special challenge: How does one live with the pressures to find "happiness for me" while making commitments to others? How can we go beyond "me" in today's world?

In marrying today, it is necessary to make thoughtful choices. If it is a stable, long relationship you want, intimacy that grows, a nurturing home, a supportive family, these are things to be given priority and worked for. None of them just happen. They have to be created by your choices, by making "we" decisions, by discovering happiness by means of your relationships. It also means working hard to build the marriage you want, with little support and few guidelines from the culture we live in.

It is also important to realize that marrying today has many great "pluses." Once one makes a decision to go beyond self, to give up "me" as the sole goal, there is great freedom to go beyond learned roles in showing love, in answering to another's needs, in sharing responsibility, in finding happiness as intimacy develops. Today's choices also offer us great freedom to love well.

Living Together: Why Marry?

More and more young couples are living together today without marriage. In 1978, more than one and a half million men and women, many under twenty-five, chose to live together, an increase of 14 percent in one year.

As this happened, sociologists looked for reasons. Some wondered if this trend suggested disillusionment with marriage, or if it was too hard to make commitments today. Or was it a protest against traditional institutions? or a new style of courtship? Some wondered if it would become a permanent substitute for marriage.

But the phenomenon of couples living together is not as extensive or common as it may seem. Nor is it replacing marriage as some have predicted. Alongside the statistics regarding unmarried couples, forty-eight million men and women have chosen traditional married household arrangements.

Both living together without marriage and marriage are happening in a time, however, when, as one psychiatrist put it, "there's still a lot of anxiety in society" about relationships. Young persons live together for different reasons. Some look at marriage with new fears, are hesitant to commit themselves for life. Lifestyles of friends, uncertainties in the economy, a feeling that no person or thing can be depended on for long—all act as subtle pressures to choose a short-term relationship.

Some simply want to meet what they believe are their needs now: they are unconcerned with the future.

Clearly, of couples who live together, some want a sexual relationship, some want companionship, some reject marriage. Of those who relate it to marriage, some want to test a relationship before marriage, and others live together in hopes of building affection into real readiness for marriage and commitment. Some couples want merely to escape an unpleasant family situation or personal problems.

The question of right and wrong involves other questions: What is "right" for persons looking for real growth in loving one another? Does living with another without marriage help or hurt persons in meeting basic needs for intimacy, trust, love, and in building a lasting relationship?

Researchers are asking many questions about relationships today. A study of 151 couples divided the couples into three groups: couples who lived together outside marriage, those who married after cohabitating, those who did not live together before marriage. The study revealed that the cohabitating female subjects rated their "personal dedication to continue living with their partner," as highly as did married females. The cohabitating males, however, rated their own dedication "significantly lower" than married males did. This research suggests that there may be fundamental differences in the levels of commitment and motivations of unmarried men and women living together.

One researcher says that she and an associate found in a study that "when people know they are going to be committed to each other for a certain length of time . . . their attraction to each other increases, their perception of each other changes, and as a consequence, their behavior toward one another changes."

Given what was presented in an earlier chapter regarding the Church's view of sex, it can come as no surprise that the Church has always taught that living as a couple outside of marriage is wrong. Non-marital sexual relationships are decisions to make short-term commitments or even decisions **not** to make emotional commitments at all. In either case, one or both of the persons are holding a portion of themselves back. Yet, as was mentioned earlier, sex involves all of who we are—body, mind, emotions, and spirit. It is a mistake to pretend or assume that it can be limited to a merely physical or intellectual matter. Secondly, sex includes the possibility of conception, pregnancy, and new life. Non-marital relationships offer no support for family life and no commitment to parenting.

Father Gregory Kenny, CMF, sums up the matter this way: "I think the fact that they are not ready to announce their marriage publicly— whether it's because they 'can't afford to be married now,' or 'have to finish school,' or whatever other external reason—is an indication that their relationship lacks the depth necessary for marriage and the intimate sharing it involves."

The following interview is one couple's experience of living together. As you read it, ask yourself: Is living together different from marriage? What promotes intimacy and makes it last?

An Interview with Marti

Marti and Ron, a happily married couple in their thirties, lived together for a year as college students before they were married. Marti reflects on those early days of their relationship.

Why did you start living together, Marti?

I don't know. There was never a conscious decision, we just did, and no one knew about it. I had just broken a two-year engagement with someone else. Ron had been deeply hurt too. I wanted the warmth and neat things of a relationship and was scared to death to go without them. Ron introduced me to many things and the Vietnam War movement. Also, it was the first time I'd spent with a man who was smarter than myself.

As you look back, Marti, was living together different from marriage?

Well, part of it is you don't make a commitment to one another. Living together is a situation where either one of you can walk away at any time. I am now a secure person, but at that time I wasn't and that was very difficult for me . . . to realize that I could invest a lot of time and energy in the relationship, in making it work, and he could walk at any time. I never felt like I would be the one to walk, and he never felt he would be the one to walk, but it was always there.

When you began, you weren't looking ahead. When did you worry he would leave?

Well, back then I don't think I would have done anything to promote the relationship if he wanted to leave. It wasn't cool. You let people do what they wanted to do. All you could do was sit and hope it was going to work.

But you must have had some conscious thoughts about it?

Did I love him? Oh, yes. I knew that I loved him and I wanted to go the way he was going. I remember right before we got married thinking it probably wasn't going to last, but I was excited about getting married. It had been fun, I thought. But even deciding to get married was something we didn't plan. If Jimmie hadn't been on the way, I'm not sure we would have married. I don't think either one of us could answer that. We fell into situations. Ron asked me to marry him the night we were with his folks and mine in a room, and they were trying to figure out what they were going to do with us. My father turned to Ron and said,

"Well, what are you going to do?" And Ron said to me, "Do you want to get married?" I said, "All right."

Why did you decide that, Marti?

It was what we decided to do then . . . for as long as it lasted it was fine. Neither of us was the type of people that were going to purposely disrupt that situation. But even then I knew that I had very few expectations.

Why?

Probably more to do with my self-image.

Were you afraid to hope?

A little bit. I'd been hurt badly, you know, and he had. Marriage was a nice easy relationship without a lot of demands on either side. We enjoyed spending time together, did fun things together, we laughed a lot, and all of that.

And one important thing was that we each respected the other's mind, academic ability, and other abilities. But Ron at that point did not want a wife that was going to be very demanding or really that noticeable.

When you were married, did you feel any different?

Well, we were married at the end of January and Jimmie was born in July. Getting married didn't seem different from living together.

When we married we floated. That's what we did. Looking back I don't know if that's bad. Ron was a reactionary, very angry about social issues. He expended so much of his time being really angry, not at me, but at external things . . . he didn't want a lot of hassling from me.

So even then when we were married a commitment was not made. Well, when Jimmie came along there were demands on me . . . for the first years of marriage. But Ron admitted to me that I did not make one bit of difference to his lifestyle. I fit in, but I didn't alter or make a difference in his living. Jimmie and I were not at the top of his consciousness.

Finally we had a really bad night. I kicked him out. But by

3:00 A.M. we were together again. From that point on we worked at our relationship.

Did you make a commitment?

Both of us. Before that, not consciously . . . we both had to make a commitment to Jimmie, but not to each other. Before that we just fell into situations: Jimmie was coming, we made a decision to get married. I see so many teenagers operating on the same level I was, and I worry about them because you just fall into things . . . Well, after our blow-up, we sat down that night and said, "Is it going to work? Is it worth it? Do we want it to work? Are we going to work at it? Are we going to write it off?"

And we both said we wanted it to work. And from that time on, it worked.

How long was this after you married?

Two years. Jimmie was about a year and a half.

Was it something you had to consciously decide that you could do?

Yes. It was a commitment to make it work, forever . . . except forever is a long time, there are no absolutes.

Did making this commitment make you feel differently about your life together?

Yes. I felt that I had the right to say anything I wanted to regarding us—not to hurt him but to say what I needed to be myself. Also, I did have a right to have a say in the marriage, in our relationship now. I had the right to make demands, to expect things.

Did he feel differently?

If he were here, he would tell you how it changed for him, but I think I can remember that we were talking about this with another couple who were going through the same things, and I remember hearing him saying that he began to let me make a difference in his life, you know, that he started considering me as a focal point.

After your commitment?

Yes, the focus of his life started changing, into the family. As I'm talking I'm sounding like I had to do the changing and that's not what I intend. But I have to talk from my perspective because he's not here. It takes two people to make a relationship.

Was there a change in the way you communicated?

Definitely. I think that that must have been when the real trust started forming. That didn't just happen immediately . . . again, it's not a conscious thing. But I found myself trusting him not to leave me.

The healthiest thing was when we moved out of the university town to a small town where there were just the three of us . . . Getting away from the old situation where you have been typed and where trying to change is so hard. The commitment mostly let me put down some conditions on what and how our life together was possible to me.

Has marriage been a freeing thing or a restrictive thing?

It was freeing once the commitment was made, once the relationship developed. Not before, I don't think so, you aren't yourself, I don't know that you're free to be yourself . . . not that we tried to build a false image, Ron would never allow that, but commitment was deciding to make the marriage work.

Our marriage has been a great life. I hope we can maintain that, very much. Until recently I've really had very little hope for that . . . but I think that in seeing my parents' marriage going through stages, and finally now that they've retired to see them as people who enjoy each other more after retirement . . . a relationship that lasted, still has excitement, real love and real caring. I'm hopeful.

FOR REVIEW AND REFLECTION

Write a brief reaction to the interview with Marti answering these questions: Is living together different from marriage? What promotes intimacy and makes it last?

Building a Marriage 10

A divorce lawyer and marriage counselor of many years recently wrote a book about why marriages fail today.

"Almost always you marry the right person," wrote Herbert Glieberman in **Closed Marriage.** And in his book he presented the case that marriage should be "closed" because it is "worth protecting." Yet, he says, people are "brainwashed" today not to believe in marriage. Finally, by not working at it, by not complaining until little problems become too big, they decide to end it all because they are in crisis.

"Where else do we say this?" he asks. Do we say, "If I get one more flu, or am in a bad mood tomorrow, I might commit suicide?" How ridiculous, we would think. But in matters of marriage, many people draw a similar conclusion.

The solution for many, Glieberman wrote, is a matter of working at one's marriage "twenty minutes a day," of focusing on communicating and on ways of living with one another, of facing the big or little questions over which conflicts usually occur. Perhaps it is communication. Perhaps it is as minor as how we recreate or eat together. These are individual things. But, Glieberman commented, success in a marriage means developing a process of working things out **together.**

A list of the leading causes of marital discord today, tabulated from a survey of 730 marriage counselors, sheds more light on the marriage

process. Unlike past years when sex, money, and in-laws led the list, new issues have come to the top. Communication breakdown, loss of shared interests and goals, then sexual incompatibility lead the list today, followed by infidelity, the excitement or fun gone out of marriage, money, conflicts about children, alcohol or drugs, women's equality issues, and in-laws.

The leading items—communication, loss of shared interests and goals, and sex—center around the issues of who people are and how they communicate. These are matters of sharing self and discovering one another. They reflect the very process of building a marriage.

Choosing Sexual Roles

A person's sex is a biological fact, but sexual **roles** are mostly learned. Because of the rapid changes in our society today, the choosing and living of sexual roles is one of the most important issues in marriage. Anyone who marries today without becoming aware of his or her partner's search for sexual identity is like a person who boards a train without a ticket. There's very little chance of making a successful trip.

Roles mean much more than who does the dishes or who cuts the grass. Through roles we express ourselves as sexual persons. When we choose our roles, we ask ourselves, "How should the fact that I am male/female affect the way I respond right now to this particular person, male/female?" "And because of that, what should I, or should I not, be doing right now in this situation—whether it's my job, my home, in bed, or in the kitchen?"

Most of the time we act out roles unconsciously, taking them for granted because of our childhood and cultural learnings. But many human beings suffer because of some of these "learned roles"—roles which can be so fully accepted they seem "natural" and "right." Some learned roles restrict people from exploring and growing as individuals in education, work, or human involvement. Other learned roles deny people the chance to develop a fully human personality—including **both** the traits of being compassionate, passive, caring, and emotional **and** the traits of being active, achieving, dominant, and rational. Fully human men and women are all of these and express them freely.

Only with the emergence of the women's movement in the 1960s have these issues really come to the fore in our society. And as some women have become more aware of their potential, demanding full opportunity for equal education and economic opportunity, some men have begun to recognize their options for growth as well.

Roles affect marriages deeply. Do you ever remember hearing statements like "men are the head, women the heart of every home"? "Men should be the spiritual leaders, women the source of love in every Christian family"? Can you remember other statements like these?

Adages like these were taken for granted and taught as ideals or even virtues. Think of the messages they convey: men should make the decisions because they are wiser; women should be the source of affection because they are more sensitive, understanding, and loving.

Stereotyped sex roles are still a part of the education of children today. Many parents believe them unquestioningly and pass them along. A study recently showed that parents still teach that sexuality means different rules for living. Girls are taught not to act like tomboys; boys should not hug one another or be too close as friends; fathers are often "inaccessible" to their children physically and emotionally; men "rarely shed tears"; women are the primary parents regardless of whether or not they are employed outside the home.

It is men, writes Herbert Goldberg in the **Hazards of Being Male,** who are raised to imitate their absent fathers and whose energies are caught up in the struggle to compete, achieve, and succeed in a male world where emotion and admission of failure are considered feminine.

Men have learned to "bond" with other males, "to make money, to sport, to fraternize" wrote Phyllis Chesler, author of **About Men.** They learn early in childhood to expect less emotional involvement with their fathers than their mothers. It is on women, she believes, that men learn to depend for "emotional and physical relief or safety, intimacy, human warmth . . ."

The stereotyped role of women has been that women are the nurturers, the providers of human needs—passive, finding happiness in serving, always being there to reassure and understand. Women were not expected to compete, achieve leadership or excellence in sports, professions, business, or government.

It is these learned, unconscious roles which ultimately turn men and women against one another, unhappy with relationships in which neither are allowed to become fully human. Yet, in living them, few people can understand that it is the role, not the person, which is preventing them from opening up to real needs and feelings of the other. It is also, says Goldberg, the pursuit of the "masculine" role of success and competition which kills men at an early age, or drives them to divorce or to alcohol or to other women. Yet, despite these stereotypes, few men and women really fit all the traits thought of as "masculine" or "feminine." Think of people you know. How many "masculine" women do you know who are rational, aggressive, dominant persons? How many men do you know who are passive, sensitive to others, emotional and expressive persons? Do these traits lessen or improve their ability to love, to work, to be happy human beings?

When we describe a well-rounded person, we usually include an abundance of traits that combine both "femininity" and "masculinity" no matter what the sex of the person involved is. Human beings come in all types, but everyone is called to develop both sides of personality, passive as well as active. It seems as though our common sense tells us that a good person is a blend of both. Yet in our marriages and work situations we think very much in terms of roles.

In high school, roles affect friendships: "I go with a girl," confided a seventeen-year-old to a parent, "because it's the only way I can really be myself, can really talk about how I feel." Adolescent boys learn to turn to girls for friendship, to share feelings, fears, emotions. They tend to compete and share accomplishments with other boys, however.

The lessons carry through to marriage: men learn being male is not to be feminine. Men don't cry, don't show fear, need an "excuse" to

get together with another man. Images of male "macho" and success are fed to us through the media, ads, practices of the business world, economic patterns of paying and hiring, promoting men more than women. We come to see these images as natural and carry them over into our concepts of ourselves, even into our relationships.

Herb Goldberg paints vivid pictures of the roles that many pursue in marriage. He describes a typical couple who fall in love, marry, and spend years doing what they have been taught brings happiness to themselves and to each other. Husbands work long hours, usually away from the home, under pressure to succeed financially and to establish some degree of social status. Wives at home are totally occupied with managing the household, parenting children, perhaps working outside also, being helpmate, nurturing full-time, and believing themselves responsible for the happiness of husband and children. Both spouses accept this lifestyle, believing this is how good husbands and wives should live.

Yet as one woman expressed it, "We were doing all the things we thought we were supposed to, not wanting to be disagreeable, until we found we didn't have anything to share anymore."

Another put it this way: "We get married, live the way we've been taught, and suddenly there're problems. No one prepared us for this!"

Problems in living learned sexual roles are the cause of many conflicts in relationships. One woman told her story this way: "I was married fifteen years, a typical housewife in a typical neighborhood. He worked, I raised the children. We didn't share real friendship, but neither did any other couple I knew.

"Finally when I needed to work and wanted to do repair jobs, we clashed. I wanted to be a carpenter—I'd always wanted to work with wood. But he hit the ceiling—it was an insult, an affront to his masculinity!"

A fifty-year-old man talked about his marriage this way: "We married, raised a family. I worked hard and long, but my job was really a pressure job. I started drinking to unwind. When I started drinking at lunch I knew it was time to quit. I got a job which paid less but which let me be a human being.

"Well, Betty never liked the fact I made a lot less money. She thought I'd let her and the kids down, kept trying to talk me into getting a job where I'd 'use my talents.' So I finally left her. She kept thinking it was me who had to make her happy. But, you know, no one could make her happy. She'd always figure it was up to somebody else."

In successful relationships **both** people develop a willingness to ask whether their real needs are being met, how they feel about their sexual roles, and how they want to live differently.

The conflicts and choices about sexual roles are summarized clearly in a poem titled "For Every Woman" by Nancy R. Smith:

For every woman who is tired of acting weak when she knows she is strong, there is a man who is tired of appearing strong when he feels vulnerable.

For every woman who is tired of acting dumb, there is a man who is burdened with the constant expectation of "knowing everything."

For every woman who is tired of being called "an emotional female," there is a man who is denied the right to weep and to be gentle.

For every woman who is called unfeminine when she competes, there is a man for whom competition is the only way to prove his masculinity.

For every woman who is tired of being a sex object, there is a man who must worry about his potency.

For every woman who feels "tied down" by her children, there is a man who is denied the full pleasures of shared parenthood.

For every woman who is denied meaningful employment or equal pay, there is a man who must bear full financial responsibility for another human being.

For every woman who was not taught the intricacies of an automobile, there is a man who was not taught the satisfactions of cooking.

For every woman who takes a step toward her own liberation, there is a man who finds the way to freedom has been made a little easier.

Communication: Sharing Who We Are

When talking about marriage today, we hear over and over the phrase, "Communication is the key." But few people enter marriage aware of the need for good communication skills. Dr. Sidney Jourard summarized it this way: "Perfectly good marriages are ended because something has gone wrong. Actually, I should say they are ended right at the point where they could begin." What they have uncovered about each other is the truth, Jourard continued, and the question really is: Is marriage something in which two people continue to hide themselves, exercise power, or is it "a commitment to dialogue? Failure to dialogue is the crisis of our time, whether it be between nation and nation, us and them, or you and me."

In Jourard's view, a crisis in marriage is often the beginning, the recognition that both have come to see that indeed they are different from each other, somehow so different that talking must begin. But many see this as an end, and go no further together, missing the chance for new life together. Think back to the crisis Marti and Ron went through, described in the last chapter.

Most couples do not communicate well. Two people who have written widely on marriages today believe that **on the average there is only a half hour of good conversation each week between a husband and wife.**

One director of a Marriage and Family Counseling Center serving urban and rural couples describes it this way: "It's not that people don't talk, but it's what they talk about—not the gut issues, their emotional feelings, the more personal problems. And because of the pace at which they live, the lack of communication skills or the time to learn them, people live making a lot of assumptions about each other until the thing just blows!"

When we learn to communicate, we learn to overcome unreal expectations. Two family therapists discussed causes of marital problems, tracing the relationship between good communication and realistic ideas of marriage. "We married, and our children still marry with the idea that a good marriage means no conflict. Our society pressures us still more to look to marriage for everything today: joy, companionship, sex, love, caring, fun—we expect it all in marriage. But no relationship can provide everything, perfectly. It's impossible. So a husband and wife clash and suddenly think, 'We've got a bad marriage here.' "

"And when they do clash," responded her associate who works with teenagers, "they frequently don't have the skills to work out their differences. Commitment is there, and they care about their marriage, but somehow there isn't a patience. There's a feeling in the air today that 'I'm going to do it my way. I want to have what I want, and I want it now.' And they don't know that marriage has to be worked at. No one ever told them that.

"How could we learn?" she asked. "In our own homes all we saw was the fights—if our own parents clashed. Usually when problems were worked out, it was done privately. We never knew what happened, or how they began to communicate. And in one-parent homes today, I see kids who have even greater unrealistic expectations of what a good marriage relationship is; if they haven't lived in a good marriage, they often have very unrealistic ideas, myths, about how perfect a good marriage must be."

Realistic, honest communication is a process of discovery of two people about one another. It demands skills and certain assumptions.

1) **The first step requires that the marriage commitment is one based on trust and acceptance of one another.** No one works to save a relationship without a decision to make it work. Neither does a person take real risks to reveal things to another without the trust that it will not mean anger or rejection. As mentioned in an earlier chapter, intimacy springs from the confidence that what is hidden can separate us; that what is revealed can ultimately draw us closer.

2) **Good communication presumes realistic expectations about what marriage should be.** In the words of the two therapists, it means knowing that no marriage is perfect and expecting that a good life together requires hard work and patience.

3) **Good communication springs from a "democratic" family.** In the words of one therapist, good communication is based on mutual respect for one another. If we look on another as an equal, someone with dignity who deserves respect, we are more prepared to accept that person's right to his or her own feelings and ideas. (But if we're involved in a power relationship, a "consumer-relationship" where we expect that person to respond in a certain way to us, to fulfill certain needs of our own, communication is undermined.)

For example, the wife who expected her husband to provide her with a certain income is not willing to listen to his feelings about why he wanted a lower paying job. The husband who needed to see his wife doing "woman's" work because her wood-working threatened his own feelings of masculinity was not receptive to hearing her feelings about work and personal growth.

4) **Good communication takes time.** The marriage relationship becomes richer through time as each partner takes risks and reveals himself or herself. It is impeded by an outlook taught by the media and pop psychology that we need "to take care of ourselves first, and take what we need now," in the words of one therapist. Consequently, many people give up too soon.

5) **Good communication involves learning skills.** There are excellent courses which teach people how to communicate. Workshops, marriage encounter groups, and marriage counselors are all sources for couples who want to acquire communication skills. Many aspects of marriage are involved. Among them—to list a few—are the following steps:

---

1) Identify your own feelings and don't feel guilty about them.
2) Clearly tell your spouse what your feelings are. Learn to accept the feelings he or she reveals to you, realizing they are not the same as behavior.
3) Learn that no one else can make you happy. Don't expect every communication to be a source of happiness for you either.

4) Recognize that as adults we're still carrying with us the remnants of our feelings of childish fear, anxieties, repressions.

5) Expect change in another. Don't be threatened by change, differences.

6) Work at conflicts to identify some common points of agreement. Build from there.

7) Try to show an accepting attitude toward the other; be nurturing.

8) Communicate about the issue at hand; don't generalize; try to be thoughtful in the way you lay out feelings that are hard to accept.

9) Be a good listener. Don't start thinking about your response until you've finished listening to what he or she has said.

10) Realize decision-making must be mutual, "democratic." It must be approached with attitudes of mutual respect for one another.

Finally, when we care deeply for another person, nothing speaks more profoundly than the intimate, universal language of touch. Touch, beginning with the earliest caress from mother or father, is what first communicated we were lovable. Touch was our earliest link to humanity. Touch, if we keep it honest, is a most powerful sign of total love and giving—with meaning building up from the simple touch all the way to sexual intercourse.

When touch is honest and we can trust what it seems to say, it expresses human love, giving, affection for one another. Touch which means intimacy and commitment in a sexual relationship is the most powerful human communication.

Pleasurable, communicating touch helps husband and wife reaffirm their trust in each other and renew their commitment. Touching can have powerful meaning if it doesn't just mean "I want intercourse now," making the other feel used. When it does not begin and end in bed, touch can build acceptance, security, love. It can be an intimate dialogue.

What is that dialogue? It can be her touching his face in the morning, his hugging her on seeing her at the end of the day, touches which spontaneously say "I care." Sexual caresses which are isolated, not part of this kind of dialogue can prevent or damage love.

Sharing Values:
Building a Stable Core in a Changing Marriage

"What hasn't changed in our lives?" she asked him as they walked slowly in the cool summer night.

"What do you mean?" he asked. "We're still married, aren't we?"

"Well, almost everything about us has changed. We've changed jobs, cities, houses. We've had children and they're starting to leave; we've changed in looks, interests, friends. What's left to change before we aren't us anymore?"

"Not much," he said. "But we're still us—as long as we share the things we believe in, I guess."

A marriage that carries two people through time can take on many new faces. Like a river it can change in current, in setting, in direction. What is it that remains the same, giving stability, a sense of permanence through it all?

Essentially two things must remain the same: (1) the chosen commitment based on love, and (2) the mutual choosing and sharing of the values by which the two link the future to the past, find meaning in what they do. All else can change. But when two people no longer share mutual values in important things, no meaningful life is possible between them.

The important values which bind a marriage center in four areas:

1) **shared values about their marriage—a friendship as well as a sexual relationship**
2) **shared values about the money and goods they share**
3) **shared values about their relationship to God and others**
4) **shared values about sex**

As you read about these critical values, think of ways that a dating couple can discover each other's values **before** marriage.

TAKING CARE OF THE MARRIAGE RELATIONSHIP

Many men and women are becoming more aware of the need to go beyond learned roles in building a loving marriage relationship. One effect of this is a movement toward marriages based on nurturing friendship. Today a husband and wife are freer to see one another as the persons they are, not merely roles they fill. A couple who can do this is well on the road toward building friendship.

It is friendship, in essence, which ultimately must carry a couple through the changes they meet in marriage, the struggles to communicate, the duties they share, and into the aging years. After the "honeymoon stage," it is friendship which must take over if a marriage is to bring the happiness and richness sought in a shared life.

"When you're first married it's such a sexual thing," commented Joan about her early years of marriage. "And after that period was over I came to find that I almost hated Dan. But what happened was that I learned to love him."

A pastor described a woman who had been to see him a few days before: "She was in here for counseling about a divorce. She felt she had to do it. But she explained, 'If only my husband had been kinder to me, I could have learned to love him, as my sister learned to love her husband.' "

What both women are describing is the struggle to build a new relationship in place of what was only a sexual one. If a couple are not friends when they marry, they need to build a friendship later. Nothing else can carry them happily through a lifetime of shared living.

But in our society we seldom equate our notion of love with what we know about friendship. A friendship in marriage, like any other friendship we have, needs to be valued and cared for. It deserves priority

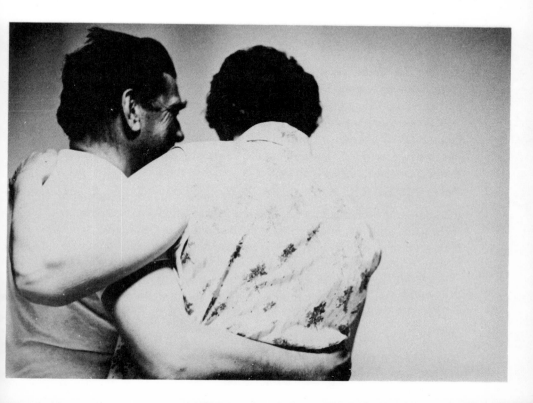

treatment. It requires time to care for it, reflection about how to maintain it. In the words of Herbert Glieberman, it's "worth protecting."

What are the qualities of a good friendship? Think of your friendships regardless of sex. When sexual aspects are eliminated, what is a real friendship?

Good friends see one another as equals. We all can think of false friends who we felt used us or depended on us for everything. We could not really be ourselves with those friends, those "consumer relationships."

Good friends know we are not perfect. We understand we don't have to be. There is a feeling when we are together that they accept us and respect us. And there is a feeling of freedom to be ourselves.

Moreover, good friends rejoice in the good things that happen to us. We know they are not jealous of us or threatened by our successes, fearful of losing us. We can bring our good news to them and celebrate together. We can talk about our shortcomings comfortably and with humor.

Good friends find us interesting, fun to be with, and they can relax when they are with us. We also find our friends interesting, fun to be with, relaxing. In simple words, friends like each other. They are people we find to be independent—with a life of their own. Often we find friends intriguing, slightly mysterious.

We can count on a good friend to be honest with us. A good friend will tell us when we are wrong and we allow them to be candid and frank. We do not need them as our "cheerleader."

Think of other things you experience with a good friend. Do you find that most often your good friends are of your own sex? Very often the roles we learn for male and female train us to relate to members of the opposite sex, not as friends, but in terms of roles.

Much of the cynicism we see today comes from the assumption that men and women cannot be friends. People who have been hurt in love, who have experienced sex as dishonest or separated from friendship and real intimacy, come to believe that sex and supportive human relationships are necessarily separate.

Couples who cherish the relationship of marriage, then, care for it, giving it the priority they would a good friendship. It means working for:

1) *Making each other primary:* in sexuality and friendship we are first of all close to one another. Yet it cannot be a suffocating, "no one else" relationship excluding all other friends, interests, independent life outside marriage. It means instead working for the fine line of being "first" to each other.

2) *Valuing the relationship:* make time for private recreation as well as communication. Plan time together regularly which does not always involve doing "useful" things. "Waste time" together, try to think of new ways to have fun together, so that time spent is a renewal. "Take time out to play when you get married," said an older woman to a young bride. "That's my one piece of advice. Choose your main sources of recreation as things you can enjoy together."

   "What we often see," said a director of a center for the separated and divorced, "is couples who have no time or energy left for each other and their relationship. If you value a relationship, you've got to take care of it. What's the key task of a relationship? It's planning it, taking it seriously, 'managing it,' even if it includes planning new rituals along the way to celebrate shared life along the way of change."

3) *Develop a sense of humor about the relationship:* "Nothing would have pulled us through if we didn't laugh," said Jack about his eight-year marriage. "But laughing, making a joke, is really a big thing to me. It helps you get through the ordinary things that can get you down and helps remind you of what this is all about. It helps us remember why we're in this together and how much we share."

SHARING VALUES ABOUT MONEY AND GOODS

In a recent survey of 3,900 married men and women, "money" was listed with lack of communication as a major problem in nearly half of American marriages. Money has always been considered one of the top three causes of marital problems. Regardless of the box score, we know that money and finances are critical issues in every marriage, for they stand for more than wealth: how money is earned, handled, and valued represent key values in a marriage.

To those who have earned them, money and goods may mean the following: "This is the fruit of my labor, what I've invested so much of my life in. If you waste it, you reject part of me." Money can represent power in a relationship. The husband who puts his wife on a budget, demanding an account of "his" money for "her" purchases—made really for the family—is using money to exercise power, a value he wants in their relationship.

The wife who evaluates her husband's work in terms of the money he earns makes it a key value overriding other considerations in his work choice. The couple who chooses not to have children in order mainly to live on two full-time salaries is using money as a value and goal. It is more than a means to live; it is a life goal.

Money problems, like sexual problems, can be symptoms of deeper marital problems. They can reflect poor communication, resentment over roles, unhappiness with the other's value system, the exercise of power in the relationship, or simply the poor understanding of mathematics and finances. The last is a simple matter in terms of the marriage relationship, but the problems it creates can be just as serious.

Regardless of the cause, money conflicts become even more serious with inflation, increasing unemployment, and diminishing resources. Any couple marrying today must be realistic about the importance of having similar values about earning, spending, and handling money. In the years just ahead, decisions about money will affect everything in the marital relationship. "Will we have children?" often becomes a question of "Can we afford to?" "Whose job comes first?" involves not only how much money we earn but how we live sexual roles, make decisions, share power in the marriage. "How much will you work?" is a question which not only involves money but how parenting will be shared, how much money we will earn, and how our children will be cared for in or out of the house.

Other questions about money are:

1) **Is money to be ours, or yours and mine?** This question reflects the views and values about commitment, marriage as a "we" relationship of trust.

2) **Who handles the money?** Often people marry with assumptions from their own upbringing that handling money reflects power or certain sexual roles—such as duty—in the marriage. All of these assumptions should be talked out. The decision as to who handles the money should be made mutually, done on the basis of what works best,

what pleases most. The money decisions which work and which are "we" decisions are good decisions.

3) **What kind of lifestyle do we want to live?** How important are wealth and nice things in our life? These are perhaps the most critical questions in a marriage relationship in the coming years. As goods increase in cost, couples who place the highest values on material goods will face some of the greatest pressures in their marriages.

4) **Are we earning enough to survive?** If not, are we mishandling money or deficient in skills? These questions are among the most critical in many marriages today, for millions of Americans live on the edge of survival.

It is difficult to find joy in a relationship when the couple must struggle against continual financial problems. Many marriages end because of the problems of poverty. If economic pressures increase, more and more couples will ask whether their worries come from insufficient money, poor management, or ignorance. It is here that any weaknesses in the marriage relationship come to the fore: communication problems prevent airing feelings, needs, real discussion, and good decision-making; roles which work against the nurturing of one another perpetuate resentments, unhappiness, misuse of power—all of which surface in times of financial stress.

Any marriage which works needs the following skills and attitudes:

1) **Before or early in marriage, talk honestly about learned attitudes toward earning, handling, and valuing money.** "How do I feel? Where are we alike? Where are we different? On what common ground can we agree?" Take nothing for granted.

2) **Learn bookkeeping, banking, and other necessary financial skills.** Choose mutually, in a democratic way, who should handle the money. Talk about problems together.

3) **Discuss the values which are most important in a shared life.** Is it what we do, why we live, or what we own that is most important to us? How do we decide priorities when increasing costs of goods and energy cut into our income? What is most important to our happiness? Why?

Couples who fail to deal with these questions or postpone conflicts on these issues are drifting toward marital disaster. In the coming decades money and spending choices will be critical choices that either bring husbands and wives closer or wedge them farther apart.

SHARING VALUES ABOUT GOD AND OTHERS

The ability to give is the measure of the Christian life. Christ talks simply about who shall be saved: those who have shared and served others.

Many people who marry never mature enough to want to share. Their growth is stunted psychologically and spiritually, and their marriages reflect this. The values they pursue as couples reflect absorption in themselves.

But many other couples bring maturity to marriage, or grow to it as a couple. These people live a married life which reflects generosity and a desire to share the love and values they have with others. Their life brings joy and a sense of meaning to the marriage itself: "What **we** are going to do with our lives is worthwhile." This knowledge brings them closer, helps them survive change and problems which could devastate another marriage.

How a couple live a generous life is a matter of choice, a value which should come by the conscious decisions they make. Sharing can take many forms.

1) **Marriage—a covenant, not a contract.** A leading rock star told reporters shortly before his wedding, "I love my bride. But, yes, it's true that our lawyers have been meeting right up to the hour over our agreement on property rights. After all, who can be sure of anything these days? If we only stay married six months, she's not getting half my property!"

The rock star was talking about his marriage as if it were a **contractual** arrangement and nothing more. A **contract** is a legal tool which sets out the conditions or limits of the agreement being made. Contracts stress the limited or temporary nature of the agreement. People make contracts with others at any age. A child might say to another child, for instance: "I will do such and such if you will do such and such."

A **covenant,** on the other hand, is a very different kind of agreement. At the Second Vatican Council, Church leaders studied the sacrament of marriage and its meaning in today's world. After careful debate, the participants chose to use the word **covenant** over **contract** in a document regarding marriage which has been described as "perhaps the most characteristic achievement" of that Council. Marriage, they said, is deeply affected by changes in the world today, but its essential character remains the same: "rooted in the conjugal covenant of irrevocable personal consent."

In selecting the word **covenant** over **contract,** the Church leaders chose a freer word, suggesting fewer limits to a relationship. A covenant is an agreement between persons which implies friendship and which expresses commitment, not conditions. Covenants range in purpose from the extremely serious yet innocent covenants children make in joining into secret clubs all the way to the great covenant in Scripture made on Mount Sinai between God and the Hebrew people.

In all covenants, there is a promise made. In marriage, it is this: "spouses mutually bestow and accept each other" in their "many-faceted love," reflecting God's love in their lives. They promise to belong to each other in love all their lives.

2) **Parenting—as natural parents or adoptive parents.** Parenting is a serious lifelong commitment to service not to be taken lightly. Children have a right to be loved and cared for. They need a relationship which is nurturing, giving. People who have children in order to enjoy them are often surprised: childrearing can be difficult, even

divisive. It involves great amounts of giving, periods of difficulty, sacrifice, and self-doubt, as well as times of great satisfaction, joy, shared happiness. It's not for people who still need to grow up themselves. Yet immature people who become parents can find being parents matures them.

Decisions to parent need to be mutually made—with realism about today's world. There are few rewards from society today for parenting, especially for women; women or men who stay home to care for their children find little support from the culture. Families who raise children while both parents work full-time face great difficulties in dealing with the pressures and the pace of living, spending time on close relationships in the family, and finding good childcare. All of these issues need the serious thought of both parents. Children need to grow up in an atmosphere of love, with realistic expectations of where the joys of parenthood are to be found. For those parents willing to make the commitment, able to give love, who place a high value on the child given to them, the rewards are rich indeed.

3) **Community Service.** Couples can make a conscious decision they will live lives of sharing service to the community. A couple who share this value find new things in common as they become more involved in that pursuit. If they have some kind of unity, problems can be more easily surmounted: they have the resources to deal with time away from home, money problems. But if the activities of one seem worthless to the other, then these things can be a source of conflict. If one person has certain values—such as community service or a job serving others or political involvement, for example—it is very important to talk about these values with the other, and to work toward acting on them. A couple who share such values can focus outward, beyond themselves, living their marriage as a source of strength, a refuge for others. A couple who think only of their own immediate needs face the world like a fortress, closed against the inevitable assaults of time and change. The first view promotes growth, openness in the marriage; the second puts it on the defensive, prevents growth, kills generosity.

The decision to serve in some way is the decision of a husband and wife to reach beyond themselves, whether it involves children or service, which is parenting in another form. Within this kind of value system they learn to reach out to the needs of friends, community, or nation, in ever widening circles.

SHARING VALUES ABOUT SEX

It is in sexual love that husband and wife can experience the heights of emotion. Sexual love brings absorbing pleasure to a marriage. A husband and wife can give themselves up to it, identify with it, share powerful emotions, and be satisfied together. Finally, those feelings open up husband and wife to one another, taking each out of a separate existence to immerse them in mutual joy and pleasure.

For many couples—caught in pressures, pace, worries of building family in changing times—sex may be one of the few effective ways of gaining this aspect of love. A good sexual relationship allows husband and wife to move past their differences in a way that no other unity can.

All of us grow up learning that sex is an important part of life. Today, however, young lovers often approach marriage with unrealistic expectations of a good sexual relationship, because they are victims of many sexual myths of our times.

More couples today who find sexual problems in marriage seek counseling, and doctors and therapists are seeing a different focus to the sexual problems. "While it used to be problems of simple sexual dysfunction, inability to experience or enjoy intercourse, it's now shifted to things involving the relationship," commented one sexual therapist. "We're now seeing issues of power and control relating to sex today."

A sexual relationship is a reflection of the whole relationship. So it is important to ask: what makes for a good sexual relationship in marriage?

Virginia Johnson and William Masters, a husband and wife team who have done pioneering research in human sexual response, have expressed very important ideas about the prerequisites for a good sexual relationship.

In their book **The Pleasure Bond** Masters and Johnson make a strong case for the importance of commitment in a good sexual relationship. Sex flourishes when the relationship is a "circle of commitment": being together brings happiness; the couple tries to keep each other happy to make the relationship continue; the more they try, the more happiness it brings. "They live according to the commitment of mutual concern, and pleasure is the bond between them." Being unfaithful breaks the circle, fidelity strengthens it.

There is no reason why any couple who are committed and intimate, "with a commitment secure enough to allow them to be vulnerable without fear," would not become "fully functional sexual beings." Just one other thing is necessary besides this intimate commitment, these researchers believe: it is necessary that partners think of themselves as sexual persons, understanding that their bodies are good, that a good marriage involves being responsible to one's sexual feelings, becoming comfortable with one's body.

And in the "circle of commitment" each wants to bring happiness—psychologically and physically—to the other. Viewed this way, sex in marriage is simple: a normal, natural expression of love.

Yet we marry with a lot of false expectations or myths about sex today, myths which often undermine the sexual relationship.

Myth #1:
That in a good marriage sex must always be overwhelming, exciting, perfect.

Sex is a part of marriage, and like everything in life it has its dull average days as well as its exciting ones. The only guidebook by which a couple should judge their sexual relationship is if it is pleasing, honest, growing in openness and discovery of one another. There is no standard in the sky to which every act of intercourse must conform. Happily married couples have to keep a sense of humor about everything they do. Sex, like anything else, can be taken too seriously.

Myth #2:
That it is our performance that counts.

It is not our performance but our ability to express love and acceptance that is the real turn-on in a good sexual relationship. Films, the media, sex manuals, and our consumer-oriented society have all combined to teach us the myth that sex is a technique, a skill, a matter of performing well if it is to be a pleasurable experience. Some even fear marriage for this reason. "How can I be sure I can be a good sex partner?" they come to wonder. But the only "expert" in fact is the one who conveys to the other that "it's you I totally love and accept." When a loving husband or wife takes the other in a loving embrace, whatever each one does to assure the other that sex means acceptance, love, affection, understanding, wanting to make the other happy—these are the only techniques which ultimately count in fulfilling sexual relationships.

Myth #3:

That a good sexual experience means that there should be several orgasms, that both partners should come to orgasm at once, and that both partners must come to orgasm.

What ultimately matters is the place of the sexual experience in the total sexual relationship. Masters and Johnson call this concentration on acts "turning persons into objects"; "Touch is an end in itself," they continue, not the means to an end. If the couple value touch in itself, are comfortable with their bodies, and have the mutual desire to make the other happy, they have the essential ingredients for a good sexual relationship in marriage.

An awkward first night is no problem in a marriage if real acceptance is there along with trust and a sense of humor. The trust that can be generated more than makes up for lack of experience. Two people who are clearly vulnerable, caring for one another, and open to one another's needs far surpass old notions of the active male and the passive female.

A hectic life, tension, and fatigue are all factors which affect every marital sexual relationship and the ability to have orgasm or intercourse. In Masters and Johnson's findings, even a good sexual relationship can be lost when husband and wife become significantly less involved in the other's life, placing more emphasis on other obligations, failing to make time or take privacy for their own sexual relationship or keep a sense of humor about their lives. Finally, after years of marriage with little thought spent on the marriage itself, sex becomes just another obligation—"instead of uniting them, sex separates them."

To keep a good sexual relationship, then, involves many things: commitment, trust, faithfulness, being comfortable with one's own body, valuing and taking responsibility for one's own sexual feelings, seeking the happiness of the other, and being open toward what it is that makes for that happiness and pleasure. Sex, like the marriage itself, needs to be valued and treasured.

Our values regarding sex are powerfully connected with our values regarding parenting and family, mentioned earlier. The next chapters will treat the problems people today face in creating families. And creative, alternative approaches to family life will be suggested—with which we can develop better, more humane, more Christian family situations.

FOR REVIEW AND REFLECTION

1) Write a brief reaction to the poem by Nancy R. Smith on page 121, summing up the problem with learned roles today.

2) Of the ten communication skills listed on pages 124-125, which one seems most important to you? Explain briefly.

3) Write a brief personal reaction to the idea that marriage is based primarily on friendship, not sex.

4) If you were married at this moment, how much money would you need to earn this year to support your needs and lifestyle? Compare your estimate with other students and explain how you computed it.

5) If you were writing a marriage contract, what provisions would it contain? Explain each provision briefly.

Family 11 in a Changing World

Today's Family Relationships

A few years ago, a national magazine featured a story about the family Christmas reunions of an elderly Mexican-American couple in Texas.

When the children and grandchildren of Lorene and Julian Vela come to celebrate with their parents, it is a joyous, noisy event, wrote the authors. You can almost see the love flowing from one person to another in this family. They know their family is special.

Indeed it is. Lorene Vela was arthritic and in pain at the age of forty when she took in their first child, an abandoned infant. And during the next sixteen years she and Julian, despite poverty and ill-health, adopted or took as foster children a steady stream of unwanted, lonely, loveless children—a six-year-old problem child, an unwanted illegitimate infant, four malnourished and frightened children, children half-starved or sullen—until they had adopted nine and had become foster parents to eleven more.

Today when these children return home as adults, love is there. They learned early in life what a gift it is!

What does the Vela story tell us a good family must be? Does it say families must be large or poor? Do they have to take in abandoned children? What must good families do to help us find joy in one another?

All of us want to feel joy at belonging to our families—a sense that love is there, a feeling that our family is special.

Think of your own family. What is it you like most about your family? What is it that you most wish you could have in your own family relationships? How many aspects of family life can you strip away and still have that sense of "family-ness"?

Today it is important to know what we value most in family life because many families are under stress, often unable to meet the needs of their members. Many families, who lack the Velas' joy at being a family, are without a sense of shared love. Many have problems and even break up under strain.

But family life is so important, that we need to have faith that family stress can be alleviated, that we can work to create what we want most in our own families.

Family affects relationships. This is the message that all of us know, but we sometimes forget what it means. As an international gathering of family-life specialists recently stated, the family's role is to be a "school of love." Sociologist Alice Rossi went even further, writing recently that the family along with the schools is the primary institution by which culture is passed on and built into the personalities of men and women in society.

If family then is so important for the way we live together, what is it that is at the heart of good family life? Can we hope to put it into our own families?

Many people have thought hard about this in recent years. One of them, Graham Pulkingham, head of a Scottish Christian community, visited hundreds of churches trying to renew themselves as communities. He wrote in **Sojourners** that the heart of good family life is found in putting our lives into the hands of other persons, of giving ourselves to others, placing trust in them—whether as adults to one another, or children to parents.

We do not have family problems because we live under the same roof with parents, children, brothers, sisters, or friends. We have family problems because of our limited ability to open our lives to one another, he wrote. We need family because it is in expanding this ability to share ourselves that we come alive.

Remember the Vela family? They literally stayed alive because two persons gave their lives over to the care and nurture of unwanted children. Every Vela learned this, trusted, and loved family because of it.

Each of us wants to believe in the goodness and strength of our own families, or our own future families. It is much easier to build trust and love into our own families if we understand why families today face stress. First, remember what was discussed back in chapters 2 and 3 about change and society and about the powerful effects of our economic system on relationships. Many of the problems families face today can be understood in light of those same factors.

1) Today's family is clearly under stress.

2) Society offers us unreal expectations for family living.

3) Society doesn't reward nurturing family living, nurturing family relationships.

4) The family we know is stripped of many functions, isolated, and expected to be self-sufficient.

5) The economy creates great stress for many families, rendering them less able to control their own future.

Today's Family Is Under Stress. The typical family functions differently than most of us expect it to because it is under stress. This stress shows up in alcoholism, family problems, and divorce. Current divorce statistics have prompted Census Bureau analysts to project that 45 percent of all children born in 1977 will become members of one-parent families at some point before growing up. Does this statistic bother you? How does it make you feel about the future of the family?

Many people are disturbed by this statistic. Some say the traditional family, as we know it, is ending. This can be upsetting for those who hope for strong and happy marriages of their own. But it should be added immediately that predictions that the family is finished are misleading. The fact that there are large numbers of single-parent families does not mean families are going to disappear. Back in 1890, 33 of every 100 marriages (33 percent) ended each year, mostly by death or abandonment. Single-parenthood is not new in America. The causes **are** new, however. The family is adjusting to changes including much longer life-span, mid-life changes, new isolation in our lives, new economic stresses.

In addition, divorce statistics are misleading. They do not tell us the number of couples who stay married, nor the age of those being divorced. Many divorces occur among younger persons, and those married earliest are earliest divorced, according to sociologist Evelyn Duvall. Those with more income and education divorce less.

Society Offers Us Unreal Expectations. Many of us have a false image of happy family life, believing that family only comes in one form: **nuclear** family (that is, the traditional, isolated family unit consisting of breadwinning father, homemaking mother, and children). But family today comes in three forms: nuclear, the single-parent family, and the extended family—consisting of singles or couples sharing a household or living with parents or relatives.

It is unrealistic today to expect every family to be the nuclear family, or to believe a good family life cannot exist except as a nuclear family. For the first time in history, the nuclear family is no longer the majority of households in our society: more than half of all households consist of one or two people. The Census Bureau predicts that by 1995 there will be many more households than today, but of smaller size, averaging two to three persons. Thirty percent of these will be single persons or households shared by non-relatives.

Is this prediction surprising to you? What kind of household do you hope to be living in in 1995? Do you see reasons why it is important to understand just what qualities make any group of people a family?

Also, many of us have false expectations for what family should do for us. As we will see later, family has changed from a unit in which

persons come together expecting to help one another, to a unit in which persons come together expecting to be made happy, emotionally renewed. Unconsciously, many of us consequently expect families to perform miracles all by themselves: to dissolve all the stress we feel in a competitive, impersonal society. We tend to blame our families for failing to make us happy, when it is we ourselves who have that life task.

Society Does Not Reward Nurturing Family Life. Do you remember the discussion in chapter 2 of society's influence on our relationships? Our technology and economy have shaped a society which encourages separation, not connectedness. In it, we are compelled to seek happiness as individuals, apart from our relationships. In order to keep our economy expanding, we are encouraged to seek continuous, immediate, personal pleasure. Also, jobs in our society require highly specialized training so that few couples or families can share tasks or work together to earn a living. In our society we are not taught the important fact that fulfillment comes from putting ourselves in the hands of others, as Graham Pulkingham described.

Traditionally our society forces men into roles in which success, power, and prestige are gained through competition. Obviously this works against their need to develop nurturing, giving relationships. Further, the great stress on work or career tends to devalue the efforts of those—women or men—who work in the home caring for children. Many people feel homemaking and childcare are not important work because they do not make money or lead to prestige.

The Family Is Stripped of Many Functions. Statistics on marriage and divorce tell only half the story. We need to understand the other half to see how family relationships can be strengthened and satisfying. Simply stated, it is not the family that is in trouble, but a certain kind of family—the nuclear family. In the words of Margaret Mead, this kind of family **should** be in trouble, for it has become an "unnatural" family. It is a family, she stated on many occasions, which has been stripped of functions and buffeted by a society lacking policies to support family life. To understand what she is talking about, we need a little history of the family.

Family life was not always what it is today. In colonial times, family life and work life were often the same: family members shared the jobs of nurturing, managing, and supporting the family. Men and women worked together in these roles without the rigid sex roles we have today. Usually families were headed by a strong father-figure on whose land, money, and authority the family was based—but women sometimes also filled that role.

Without cities, phones, and cars, the family was the main social group, even for married children established in their own homes. Families, often isolated, had to be organized, self-sufficient, and working as a group in order to survive. They learned early in life that happiness came through one's connections to the needs of the group, and they married or left to work when it fit into the needs of other family members. The family was extended, often including relatives, workers, or servants, as part of the work and social unit.

The nuclear family also existed early in our history, not just after the Industrial Revolution, as many believe. New research shows that it existed in Europe before the Industrial Revolution, but such families kept strong links to the community. This nuclear family was strong, and its flexibility made the Industrial Revolution possible, believe some historians.

Tamara Hareven, history professor at Clark University and editor of the **Journal of Family History,** believes the nuclear family has been not only subject to change but also a strong agent of change as well. Its strength has given people the ability to cope with changing times.

In an unusual essay, Hareven explained that families are not less stable today, but rather that families have been stripped of their functions and the timing and events of life have changed. We expect different things of family today, and the expectations are extreme. We have taken away most of its functions, but expect it to do more, she explained.

When the Industrial Revolution spread, for instance, men, women, and children no longer worked at home. Instead they went to work in factories, taking away the economic role of the family. When cities grew, families were no longer essential for social life. But family flexibility carried people through these changes. Today, most of the social, economic, and educational services that families once provided are gone.

There is also a different, more rigid and orderly timing to our lives. We face fewer of the drastic changes that our forebears faced, such as early death, late parenting, sudden disaster. Moreover, we come to the stages of our lives such as career choices, child bearing, mid-life, and retirement, with less help in making transitions to them. There are no close family members engaged in the same stages, to help us or to just be present with us. For example, we have more freedom to choose whom and when we shall marry, but less help in settling into married life. We have freedom to bear and raise children as we wish, but less help in adjusting to parenthood. We have more freedom to choose how we live the last years of our lives, but inadequate knowledge of what we shall do with that time.

Hareven also noted that the Industrial Revolution brought a new rigidity into sexual roles. Father's role became identified with leaving the family to earn income, and mother's with responsibility for all childcare, nurture, and home life.

Today the home is still expected to be a place of renewal. And as the work world becomes more stressful, we expect the family to make up for all that is lacking in work, community, and social life. Women, particularly, feel the burden of making everyone happy, while men, particularly, feel the burden of supporting everyone. These unrealistic roles are impossible for most people to live. For in addition to new expectations, this family is also isolated without help of a larger extended family, and without supports of community that existed earlier in

smaller towns or cities. Believing it should be successful at handling all its own emotional, social, and economic needs, people in nuclear families feel increased pressure.

It is this kind of trouble about which Margaret Mead spoke. Millions in families are suffering, she said, in an unnatural isolation. They are conditioned to believe that each and every family should be able to have a car, a nice home, good education, health care, nutrition; continue to provide the economy with unending buying power; and keep everyone happy despite the pressures of life. We have false illusions about the family, and no real public policy to support family arrangements.

The economy creates great stress for many families rendering them less able to control their own futures. Many people today are studying and writing about the economic pressures confronting the family.

Most of them speak of the many families unable to earn enough income to have access to health care and legal protection, to have control over parenting when both parents face mounting pressures to work. A quarter to one-third of all children in our society are born into families with insufficient means of housing, food, nutrition, and schooling. Margaret Mead felt that one solution is to develop public policies which support strong and nurturing family life. For example, researchers in a leading university recently concluded that the United States lags far behind France, Sweden, the two Germany's, and Hungary, in programs providing childcare or cash benefits to protect children and family life, including benefits for the working poor, maternity benefits, and housing priorities.

We will never have the **extended family of relatives** again, noted Margaret Mead, but it is essential that the policies promoting family include ways to extend family into our neighborhoods and communities, with plans for work, housing, and community organizations and services. End the isolated family, she often urged. The family is strong if we begin to recognize its importance and give it the support it needs.

Has reviewing the history of the family had any effect on the way you view problems of families today? Has it changed your ideas, in any way, of the kind of family life you hope to build for yourself someday?

All of us need family. Family problems often stem from a narrow view of what family life should be, based on false assumptions which cause dissatisfaction or guilt. But family relationships, like those of marriage, are constantly in process. We build our families. In family, as in marriage relationships, we maintain the family by valuing it and working at it. Most of all we must **want** closeness in family life, and we must **value** the people with whom we share our lives enough to give ourselves over to those persons. A willingness is needed, as Graham Pulkingham said, to put our lives in the hands of another. It means taking risks because we love.

FOR REVIEW AND REFLECTION

Write an analysis of your family, responding to the following questions:

1) Has your family suffered from the stress pressuring most families today? In what ways specifically?

2) How does your family conform to the ideal of a nuclear family?

3) Is your family able to look to relatives and friends for support? If not, why not?

Parenting Today 12

Martha and Joan: New Questions About Parenting

It was a large birthday party, one of those noisy, happy celebrations that bachelors have when they turn thirty—one of those parties at which everyone starts to feel like friends.

Martha and Joan were deep in conversation, balancing plates and glasses and trying hard to hear each other against the loud music and laughter around them. Joan, forty, had a large family. Martha, twenty-seven, and her husband Dan had been trying to decide if they would have children, as she explained to Joan. "How," she wanted to know, "does parenting affect a couple's lives and marriage?"

"We're trying to decide if we'll have a baby," Martha said, "and it's proving to be a hard decision. If we have children, we should have them within five years or it will be too late.

"I work full-time on a job that I like. I do good things for people, and I'm just beginning to be in a position where I can advance, make policy decisions. If I leave, I'll lose this chance. If we have children, I would have to quit my job, since we both would want to raise our own child, not leave it up to uncertain daycare situations—especially in the early, most formative years.

"But I feel that having children is an experience I wouldn't

want to miss in my life. It would bring a new dimension to our marriage, a new source of joy for both of us.

"Dan and I have talked about the other side of it too. We wonder about the economics of being parents. We live simply, rent a small apartment, and manage to save a little. Dan has a job which helps disadvantaged people. He likes it, but makes less money because of that. We love to travel. On our combined salaries, we make enough to take some nice trips here or abroad—but we couldn't if I weren't working.

"We're happy together now. We share a lot, both like our jobs, have money for fun together, can buy books, go to a few concerts. We eat out now and then. We've wondered how having children would change that. To have a baby now would be a lifestyle decision: we'd have to give up some of the things we like so much—and we don't know what it would bring to our marriage.

"It seems that our friends who've had children are more tied down, can't go out like they did before. One woman has isolated herself from friends, doesn't share her old interests. Is this necessary?"

What do you think of Martha and Dan's questions about parenthood? Do you think they are an unusual couple to have these questions about parenthood? Do you think you might be asking Martha and Dan's questions five, seven, or ten years from now? Why or why not?

The truth is that Martha and Dan reflect the situation of many couples today. If you marry, it will be in a social environment in which, unlike that of your parents', parenting is viewed by many as just another option of marriage.

It is very important for couples to understand this environment, to be realistic and honest about parenthood and about what they value most in their married life.

Martha's conversation reflects the changes in America which pressure couples to postpone parenthood, to postpone decisions about parenthood, or to choose not to parent at all. What are these changes? They include:

1) **The growth of technology which separates persons according to tasks and skills;** the dedication demanded for career development

makes it difficult for persons to advance if they take time off for parenting or seek flexible hours.

2) **The values of Americans, stemming from this influence of technology, which are based on work and reward, not on persons in themselves.**

3) **The widespread, permanent effects of the women's movement, which gives women, for the first time, opportunities to develop their talents and interests in employment and career outside the home, to become financially independent, to gain equal pay for equal work.**

4) **An unprecedented combination of inflation, recession, and unemployment.** This pressures many couples to continue two incomes and in many cases to fear the costs of parenting.

5) **A growing consciousness of the fragility of relationships prompts many women to develop and maintain financial independence.**

6) **The development and widespread use of birth control has created an attitude suggesting that parenthood is an option in marriage, not necessarily a part of it.**

7) **A new respect for the needs of children and their rights to love and to nurturing.** Along with this goes the fear of many couples of taking on such long-term responsibilities.

Martha and Dan, in reflecting on many of these factors, were essentially asking what it is they want most from life. Their questions suggest the greater freedom to make choices today, and the difficulty of making those choices.

Increasing numbers of couples, faced with these choices, are choosing to have children later, to postpone the choice, or not to have children at all. Many of the couples who postpone parenting finally decide not to have children. Some women, after having chosen careers, decide in mid-life to leave the job and have a baby—and find it richly satisfying.

We are living in an era different from our parents'. Some people bemoan young couples who are hesitant to become parents. "Such people are selfish," you might hear, or "a society that hates its children has no future."

It is easy to criticize too quickly, however. It is not fair to generalize about couples who do not have children. True, there are many who see responsibility and giving as a threat to personal pleasure. But many others are dedicated to advancing in careers which serve people and their communities.

Others are reacting to the difficulty of parenting in times of economic uncertainty. Still others are hesitant because they respect the needs of children and sometimes fear their own inability to meet those needs.

Two things are certain. First, no one should "fall into" parenting today. Dan and Martha do not need to become parents to have a good marriage. But whether or not they have children, they still need to be concerned with persons beyond themselves and to develop commitments to service. Some couples do this in their work, as do Dan and Martha. Some couples help other family members or friends or the community or a worthy cause. Every kind of service is a reflection of adult maturity which seeks to share what one is and has with others.

Second, sex has a primary function—the creation of human life—and families are the means by which young life is nurtured and brought to maturity. Couples who marry should give deep reflection to the responsibility to love, cherish, and care for their children.

This chapter is concerned only with couples who choose service by raising children—natural, adopted, or foster children.

How Can Joan Answer Martha?

Every child and parent relationship is different because it is affected by each person's needs, personality, and values. Joan's answer would have to be that children do not come with guarantees. They bring difficulties as well as joys. The pleasures of parenthood delight some couples and its strains discourage others. One sure answer to Martha would be, "Your life will never be the same." The following comments of two couples illustrate that parenting has unpredictable effects on a marriage relationship:

Marilyn and Jack were married five years when she found out she was pregnant. It was a shock to both of them and a threat to their lifestyle. They liked having two incomes and two careers, and had no desire to change it.

"When I found out I was pregnant, I cried and dreaded telling Jack," Marilyn explained two years later. "It was like the end of the world. We never wanted children; I enjoyed my job. We didn't want to change our lives.

"But today," she said, "Martin is a year and a half. Once we brought home this beautiful, happy kid, he worked a miracle in our lives. We hadn't wanted him, but we didn't know what we'd been missing. He's been beautiful, happy, funny, interesting. He's brought us closer together, given us more to share, brought a new center to our lives. I quit my job when he was a month old because he was sick and couldn't be taken out.

"I began a job working out of our home on a part-time basis. I see new career possibilities that enable me to take care of Martin besides or to share the responsibility with Jack. Things worked out in ways we had never imagined.

"Martin is something in our lives we couldn't live without. We never dreamed it would be this way."

Barb and Tim were married two years and always planned to have a family. Both felt Barbara, who had been a teacher for several years, should quit teaching to take care of the children. They valued their marriage relationship, worked hard to communicate better, share their thoughts and activities, and be honest with one another. They are clearly a couple whose good marriage means much to them.

But to their surprise, parenting has been a real strain on their marriage. "I miss, sometimes resent, the opportunities Tim has for outside contacts, to work with other people, to grow in his profession.

"Our children, 2 and 4, are such a hard task for me that I get depressed. I feel isolation in caring for them all day in a neighborhood where few women are home, and there are few opportunities to keep up my old interests in education. My depression is hurting our relationship.

"Sometimes I greet Tim in a bad mood, or I'm resentful of his life. It's hard on him. He feels guilty."

Each couple found parenthood different from what they expected. What can we know for sure about the effects of parenthood on a marriage? Can we know much of what it brings into the lives of a husband and wife? Couples who choose to be parents or who love and accept the responsibilities of parenting are choosing relationships as one of their highest values. As in all relationships, parenting brings with it a mixture of rich moments and happy days along with the boredom, weariness, and frustration of bad days. Like any other commitment, there are risks without guarantees: like married couples, parents embark on a shared future, certain only of their hopes, values, and love for each other. Moreover, because most people are not prepared for parenthood, there are few immediate rewards to balance the stress.

Marilyn and Jack could say a lot about the richness in parenthood. They have had few stresses so far and are able to enjoy the most important, pleasurable part of parenting—the ordinary, daily, little things which take up a parent's day, which a husband and wife can share, laugh over, and feel enriched by: laughter at seeing a child's first and easy smiles, a youngster's delight in discovering colors, food, the body, toys, animals, insects, flowers.

Parents, open to their children, without unusual stress, can get a fresh, long-forgotten look at the world through a child's eyes. They learn humility in a child's quickness to forget an irritable, short-tempered parent. They feel joy in seeing their children enjoy each other, discover their own resources, talents, and skills.

Children want to give pleasure, to be good, to love. Nurturing parents find joy in knowing their children are happy, healthy, growing, and loved. It comes in seeing a child smile in sleep, begin to play after an illness has passed, overcome loneliness. The real joys of parenthood are immensely satisfying, but easily overlooked.

Yet parenthood has another side with many burdens. The parent who is ill, over-worked, worried about money, job, nutrition, a marriage, finds it very difficult to meet the needs of children, to express love and interest in a child demanding attention. The mother who must work without adequate childcare faces constant tension and worry, guilt and doubt. Further, dispositions vary in children as well as parents: they can have demanding days, irritable, impatient days, weeks, or months. A day of tension can follow an hour of great enjoyment. Care of children, especially when there are health or financial pressures, can be a great strain—on the marriage relationship itself as well as on the adults individually. All children are essentially selfish, needing constantly to receive love.

Some couples become disillusioned when they see that marriages without children can be as happy as or better than their own. Parents who had children to fill a "hole" in their lives are vulnerable, for children cannot make them happy any more than could their spouses. The happiest parents are those who sense that life is already rich and want to share this with their children. This kind of relationship is the clearest example of nurturing love—a parent giving freely to an infant who cannot give in return.

Whether couples find parenthood a joy or a burden depends on the kind of marriage they have, their willingness to nurture, adequate money and security, a supportive environment in which to raise children, and an appreciation of the value of parenting. It presumes adequate preparation and a realism about the role of parenting.

What is the most important task of parenting? One father described it as the ability to give the child a sense of being loved, to see himself or herself as a lovable person.

"I've worked with all kinds of children who've been deprived," said Don, thirty, a father of three. "I've seen children abandoned, starved, neglected, hurt in many ways by their parents. Yet most of them loved their parents because they felt their parents loved them.

"I learned," said Don, "that my wife and I can make many

mistakes with our children and it's still all right— just so we try our best, let them know we love them through touch and in our words and actions."

Don learned what lies at the heart of good parenting: to convey to the child a sense of his or her own self-worth. It is a simple task which sometimes can be very difficult today. Sometimes it is beyond the ability of the couple in their circumstances to communicate self-worth to a child. Sometimes it requires great adjustment by the couple in living habits, roles, work, and lifestyle patterns.

Many are unprepared to meet a child's need for fully sensing his or her own self-worth. Parenthood is sudden and brings stress. Studies show that there is a drop in marital satisfaction during child-raising years of marriage. Every young couple should understand that parenting involves a transition and that most people romanticize parenting:

1) **Parenting requires a sudden transition to a new way of living for the couple.** Until a couple adjusts, parenting is often a "crisis" or a stress in the marriage, and couples least prepared for parenting face the most stress, depending on the personality and needs of the infant, and the ability of the parents to be giving, to share, and to be flexible.

2) **Parenting requires an adjustment in sexual roles.** An infant needs someone deeply involved in its care and, in America, that is usually the mother. Yet she, like her spouse, has little preparation for the immediate transition to parenthood and few guidelines for her role.

Good parenting needs a balance of "active" and "passive" characteristics: a loving, nurturing parent needs the ability to plan, manage, and train, to be firm, decisive, and sensitive, and to know much about the world and people and to make corresponding value judgments. We often think of a woman as being motherly. Yet how often do we connect men with being good fathers?

Although parenting may bring a drop in marital satisfaction, most couples are happy to do what it takes to be good parents once they accept the transition to new patterns of living. Parents have a natural ability to enjoy their children, to take pride in caring well for their children. Parenthood may be hard but, given the choice, they would not pass up the joys received from their children.

If adjustment is important in parenting, what will the eighties bring in parenting transitions? By 1990, two of every three American mothers will be holding a job, moving in a mass exodus from the home to the workplace, if experts' predictions come true.

Economist Ralph Smith, editor of **The Subtle Revolution: Women at Work,** predicts that, by 1990 only one-fourth of all American wives will be home to care for children, and 45 percent of all mothers of children under age 6 will be working for economic or social reasons. Men and women still conditioned to a certain extent in traditional "male-female" roles will be pioneers in a new world of marriage and parenting. How will they care for the children? How will this affect their lives and marriages?

In America today, wrote sociologist Alice Rossi in **The Family,** work and reward (the male role model) are more valued than the care of persons (the female role model). Consequently women as well as men are moving in the direction of the male role model—a model in which, in the past, men have been able to turn children off and on as their work schedule dictated. In the future, parents must balance male and female

qualities. Otherwise, Rossi wrote, no one will be attentive to the needs of the child. Parents of the eighties must become companions in nurture as well as in financially supporting the family.

3) **Good parenting demands realism about parenting.** Many who study the family bemoan the false expectations with which couples become parents. In 1977, E. E. LeMasters wrote in **Parents in Modern America** of the myths Americans hold about children. Much of good parenting is seeing what is needed to love and nurture children, he said, and to overcome false expectations we had in the past.

We romanticize parenthood, he continued. Too many of us think all children are "sweet and cute," that parenting is fun, that all children turn out well.

We presume that children improve marriage, that our dispositions do not play a strong role, that all children are good, and that if there are any problems it is because the adults are not as good at parenting today as in the past. We presume childless couples are unhappy, that love is enough to be good parents, that single parenting is bad in itself. But all of this is myth, noted LeMasters, and parents can be hurt when they learn these romantic presumptions about parenting are untrue.

Today, when the world needs love and relationship desperately, the quality of parenting is more important than ever before. Think of a parent who impressed you. What qualities make that parent a good parent? What qualities of good parenting draw parents closer as they raise their children? Do you know parents whose children have driven a wedge into their relationship? How did it happen?

Here is a list of qualities essential to good parenting. What would you add to it? What does it mean to you now?

---

1) **Good parents need most of all to know their task is to pass on love and a sense of self-worth—the knowledge of being loved and the ability to love—to their child. There is meaning in this task. It demands vision of a long-range goal, sometimes few immediate rewards. Parents must find satisfaction in nurturing relationships and not depend on their children to meet their own emotional needs.**

2) **Good parents need to know that raising children is not**

easy. It brings joys, stresses, and sorrows. Men and women alike need preparation—in parent education, in appreciation of family and marital communication skills, in flexibility and trust in living out the role of parents. Parent education courses should be commonplace in every high school, church, and community.

3) Good parents need to know that a loving family life is essential to parenting today. Such a life clearly demonstrates what it means to live as a Christian today: The relationship of parent to child which fosters nurturing love—that of giving oneself over to another—is the very heart of good family life, and the means by which family members enter the Christian community.

A Special Note on Contraception

Couples should discuss the specific sexual issue of birth control before their marriage. It would be hazardous for a couple to begin their sexual life together without both partners explaining their views on this matter or without coming to a mutual and conscientious decision.

Pope Paul VI in his encyclical on birth control **(Humanae Vitae)** reaffirmed the earlier position of Pope Pius XII that every act of sexual intercourse must be an expression of love and be open to procreation. He stated that all forms of **artificial** birth control are contrary to the order of nature and hence are considered sinful. In effect, this teaching says that the **only methods** of family planning open to Catholics are the **natural** methods of abstinence, rhythm, thermal, and other new experimental methods now being developed and accepted. It forbids artificial and unnatural methods. This teaching should be seriously considered by all Catholics. It is to be understood, however, that the papal position is not "of faith" nor is it infallible. It does represent a teaching authority in which the Church is guided by the Holy Spirit.

Current polls indicate that many adult Catholics do not follow the popes' teaching regarding birth control. For each married couple this is an individual matter of conscience, however. In several documents Vatican II has repeated the teaching of the Church that every person is bound to follow his or her conscience "in order that he (she) may come to God," and that everyone will be judged by his or her conscience.

In so serious a matter as considering birth control, it is obvious that a couple cannot be indifferent. Neither can they avoid making a decision by acting according to whim, pleasure, or convenience. If one is judged by God according to one's conscience, it is most urgent that he or she make conscience a true guide. As in all important situations requiring a decision it is necessary (1) to get the facts, (2) to seek advice, and (3) in relations with God, to use such spiritual means as prayer and the sacraments.

With respect to birth control, the first fact to be considered is the teaching of the pope. In addition, the following second set of facts would have to be considered by a Catholic couple: everything in their present family situation, such as the size of the family, the ages of the children, the health of the mother and father, their financial condition, and other aspects of their life together. As their decision will be judged by God, the couple will need honest communication, thoughtful prayer as well as the advice of a respected counselor who knows the teaching of the Church and who is personally acquainted with their personal and family life.

Having done all this, the couple would be in a position to decide if, because of some particular circumstances of their family life, they would be morally right in not acting in accord with the pope's teaching. They would have arrived at their decision on the basis of a tested conscience. Not to come to terms with this concern might create stress in sexual matters at a developing and vulnerable point in a marriage.

Family life brings a special challenge in the eighties. Consumer pressures place new strains on marriage and family relationships. Good family life will exist only for those who value it and work hard at it, who find the greatest rewards in the joy of a sharing family, who can move from a preoccupation with affluence to a celebration of shared life.

Families who grow together in the eighties will be those who can value persons over the pursuit of goods, money, and prestige. In a world of shrinking resources, this is the key not only to family life but to the essence of Christian living as well. Those who create the child and the home also help shape the nation and the spiritual community.

Choices of the eighties will lead many people to a new discovery of the importance of their close relationships—of the value of family life.

FOR REVIEW AND REFLECTION

Looking at the list of qualities essential to good parenting, on pages 159-160, indicate whether you agree or disagree with each item. Explain your response briefly. Add any other qualities you feel are important. Explain each addition.

Extending Family 13

Redefining "Family"

How many members are in your family?

Suppose someone were to say, "I want to pay for your family reunion. How many people will you invite?" What would you answer? one? five? fifteen? twenty? two hundred?

And what word most describes your feelings toward those you would choose to invite?

Writer Jan Howard traveled across the United States searching for answers to that question as she met, talked with, and sometimes lived with two hundred families of all kinds in researching her book, **Families.**

Her research compelled Howard to conclude, "Call it a clan, call it a network, call it a tribe, call it a family. Whatever you call it, whoever you are, you need one. You need one because you are human." Forming families is "one of the imperishable habits of the human race."

Howard's study of families went beyond the conventional, nuclear family of the breadwinning father, homemaking mother, and children. What she sought instead was a sense of "connectedness" between persons. She met few people who said they had enough of the bonds of tenderness, understanding, and support which make any group of people into a family—whether they are parents and children or just a few friends who have chosen to share housing.

Families are not dying, Howard concluded. Instead, we are changing the size, shape, and purpose of our families. Families, she added later in an interview, are simply groups of people connected to each other with enough "common history to imply a common future." She added that ideally it is a group with several age groups represented, and one we choose ourselves rather than have social agencies choose for us.

In a country where neighbors are often strangers, each one of us needs several people in our family, whether they are people with whom we live, whom we live near, or with whom we share a bond that spans the miles between. We yearn for family. It is a special event to be part of a group caught up in a feeling of togetherness.

Have you ever experienced strong, shared feelings in a group, such as at a concert, or in a group that has worked very closely on a project? Was it exhilarating to be in such a group?

We yearn for family also as a spiritual people. The essence of Christ's message is that we are members of one family under God. Jesus' role in coming was to show us how to expand our family, to overcome our feelings of separateness from one another by learning to understand our connections with others in God's family. To live this connection means to live as brother, sister, mother, father in the Christian family—loving, accepting, nurturing, helping, and sharing with other people.

The very words Christ used reflected family: "Our Father," " 'Who is my mother? Who are my brothers?' He looked over the people sitting around him and said, 'Look! Whoever does what God wants him to do is my brother, my sister, my mother.' "

Paul later summed up our family connection as no one else has: "All of you, then, are Christ's body, and each one is a part of it."

Nothing is more dominant in the Christian message than the call to expand and love our family.

So our notion of family has many dimensions.

Margaret Mead spoke often of the need to extend families. Our need, she said, if we are to survive as a people, is to create new kinds of communities—communities where people can live together mixing several generations. As a people, she repeated many times, we need public policies and private planning to help families in emergencies and in their long-range needs—learning to parent, to be married, to deal with careers.

In the years before her death in 1979, Mead traveled the country, painting for audiences a vision of new ways that public policy could create housing, neighborhoods, communities, even cities, where people of all ages and walks of life could live in clusters that supported one another, mixing generations who could learn from each other. Mixed housing could help the elderly, the young, married, and single live as neighbors. The elderly could find safety and strength. Children could see continuity in life and in their own care. Singles could love children, learn about parenting. Families in transition could find help and support.

Mead's message was that concern for children and families be given priority over economy and profit in the planning of communities. Adequate daycare, compulsory education in parenting, involvement of men in parenting their infants, bringing the elderly back into communities, environments where pregnant women will not be harmed in the work place—all of these are ways public policy could serve to expand family.

In the eighties when women will enter the work world in vast numbers, the critical needs for family preservation will be policies that support adequate family health care, nutrition, and education, affordable housing, safe work environments, and flexible scheduling to allow parents to arrange childcare.

The eighties also will be a period when America "grays," when the elderly will increase dramatically as a portion of the population. Such a process, say some, could bring the elderly closer to family, as members of expanded families. If they remain isolated, however, problems stemming from this separation will grow.

In any case, the need to expand family is a private one that each one of us shares if our own relationships are to grow and remain strong. Already persons all around us are working to do this in informal ways in the community. We see this in:

1) **resurgence of community groups of all kinds, a worldwide phenomenon**
2) **rapid growth of community newspapers**
3) **church and agency programs to form family-like groups**
4) **proliferation of support groups in every level of our lives**
5) **services to end isolation: Meals on Wheels, Adopt a**

Grandparent, Big Brother, Big Sister, single parent groups, Dial a Ride, senior citizens' groups, etc.

How many of these activities are happening in your community?

We hear stories of neighbors organizing regularly to help neighbors. For instance, the residents of a San Diego apartment complex for the elderly take part in a program to divide daily chores by joining in pairs, as "stayers" and "goers." On alternate days, each takes a turn remaining at home to do all the home tasks for both, while the other goes out to do all the outside tasks needed that day. What has developed above all is a sense of extended family in this apartment complex.

Two suburban housewives, needing to work but wanting good childcare, presented themselves to an employer as a package, each willing to do secretarial work in alternate weeks while the other cared for the children of both. "They were hesitant at first," said one, "but soon got used to it" and the plan has worked well for two years—allowing 'one even to attend college.

We see a new sense of family in the statement of a woman with small children whose marriage was breaking up: "My neighbors are my family," she reflected. "They support me when I'm discouraged, help me, share recreation, baby-sitting, open their homes with friendship and companionship to help me through these problems."

It is easy to see the seeds of sharing beginning to grow in many communities. Hopefully, this is the beginning of a new age of the extended family—one with institutions which counter loneliness and stress, which promote nurturing and joy.

Many persons want more than an informal community. Large numbers of formal communities have been established. Although the average life of a commune is one year, there are many other forms of communities, some traditional, and some peculiar to our times. Certainly community is nothing new. People have always formed communities—in tribes, clans, towns, religious communities. But today there is a resurgence of this for a broad range of reasons: economic, psychological, and spiritual.

Taking Charge, published by the Simple Living Collective of the American Friends Service Committee, describes three kinds of communities existing today for people who seek closer relationships, want support groups larger than their own family, want financial and personal help, more security, more sense of control over life, or want to live in greater harmony.

Persons who want to put one or more of these values into their lives, the book states, can put community into their lives in one of three ways:

---

1) **Share a household and daily life with others—on a permanent or temporary basis. This can be families, friends, relatives, married, or singles.**
2) **Choose to live in "neighborhoods" or particular areas to make "sharing and caring" easier.**
3) **Form communities of spirit or concern which provide support even at great distance.**

We might expand the list to add:

4) **Form associations of families or individuals who meet regularly, plan some sharing, communication, social life together as means of mutual support.**
5) **Form collectives (people joining to do a certain work together—food buying, schooling, house building).**

As we have said, people join communities for any one or more economic, psychological, or spiritual reasons. Communities can be as different from one another as two individuals. However, the essence of community has to be a strong sense of family if it is to survive. Remember Graham Pulkingham's phrase: each person must be willing to "place his or her life in the hands of others." The extent to which persons do this determines the depth of family experience shared by members.

But nothing tells us what is involved in living in community as much as the words of the persons themselves. Following are examples of three communities as described by some of the members. The first two are essentially shared households. The third is a formal, religious-based community involving sharing on the deepest level. These are not meant to be conclusive descriptions of communities. Rather they give us insight into the feelings and thoughts of persons who choose to live in extended families today.

As you read the sketches, keep these questions in mind:

1) In what ways do these people feel a "connectedness" to those they live with?
2) What were their reasons for coming together?
3) What makes the community satisfying?
4) What makes it successful?
5) What is your reaction to their lifestyle?
6) In what ways would you like to "expand family"?

The Simmons Avenue Household

(Jim Masters, thirty, has lived in a shared household the last two years with four other friends. One person owns the home and all of them share rent and living costs equally. It is a nice but simple older home in a quiet, middle-class neighborhood in a large city.)

There are many reasons I chose to do this: it's cheaper to live together. Living separately is a bias Americans have—an inordinate need for privacy, having lots of space. Many other countries aren't like this you know, and when foreign students come they're surprised, outraged, sometimes lonely with all the space given them.

So I live in a shared household to save money and then to have support and companionship. Support's a critical part of it—our culture doesn't offer much personal support.

I got into a household accidentally—I needed a place to stay. Old friends invited me in. It worked for a long time but some of us grew apart because our jobs and income and desires for living style were so different.

Now I'm moving into the idea of looking for a household on the long-term. I need that. But this means finding people a little by trial and error. First, you have to go about it with a great deal of self-searching to find people you'd like to live with.

Secondly, you have to be very clear with each other about your objectives in a house so they're readable to everyone in it. Be clear about anticipating sources of conflict, and structure life in ways that promote satisfactory relationships with everyone.

For example, at first everyone had cooking night. We came home regularly to eat together and that was really nice. But we moved to a house farther away, and the schedule fell apart. After a year, we finally realized that getting back together again, sharing meals, having cooking night was not the only way everyone could serve everyone else, but it would bring us a lot in more organized fellowship. So our meals are important when we do get together. We share our experiences, have a happy time together.

We don't share our incomes, just the expenses of living together. We don't have "yours" and "mine" on the milk-cartons. I've seen houses that did that, and they don't survive. Also I work for subsistence wages in a program combatting poverty. Our income levels are very different from one another.

We try to find sources of conflict and plan for it. On work, we have a wheel with everyone's name on it. Each week it's turned to give each of us a different job. We meet if it's necessary. We didn't meet enough before. It's necessary for people to have the same general notions, not to have any hidden agendas they want for each other; so we need to talk, air them. Married couples have the same problem.

In the final analysis, there has to be a certain amount of affection for each other, love for each other. There are people who come in it for saving money, for political work, for support, to develop simpler lifestyles or richer ones. There's no question as to how important the processes and the overall aims of people are. If you want to live a very affluent life, for example, it sets up a competitive, acquisitive program hard to maintain, pressures everyone. If you come together just to live more cheaply, that's probably not a good reason to function either. The long-term houses are those where people are there because they like each other and want to be together.

Also, our house helps us have fun together. Joy is important. Our political and economic system isn't joyful, and we need help to develop it in our lives. Watch how hard people work at having fun. They don't enjoy their lives. But we're here to help ourselves keep a balance as persons. I'm in that search for the long haul.

We need security, pleasing and joyful lives, time to be alone, reflect, meditate, have satisfying work, and many more things. Being human means learning how to love, not just my house, my work, but others.

And I keep my life simple: it allows me to have time for love, for relationships, for this kind of a life.

The Elm Lane Household

(Mary, her husband Dan, Jerry, Georgia, and Ray sat around the table in their large, cheerful kitchen. Five of seven members of a shared household, they talked about their life together in a large white frame home on a quiet street of older homes and apartments. The seven range in age from nineteen to twenty-six. Mary works for a program in global justice education. Dan works there part-time and is self-employed with Jerry in a construction business. Georgia and Ray have their own professions.)

Mary: We were old friends, and we got the idea that if we lived together, we could share expenses, enough to live the way we wanted to and do the work we wanted to, especially our interests in living simply, in a healthy way, and in doing what we could about global hunger. We had already been impressed and involved in the cooperative movement and had seen the power that comes from sharing.

Georgia: I came in for economic reasons, and I also knew I needed others to live with after having lived alone.

Dan: I lived with another person for four years, and my life was too self-centered. He and I were all that mattered. I didn't want that life any more.

Mary: We have many friends outside the house, and many visitors here. We think of each other as friends too. I don't think of us as a family, but sometimes we get along a lot better than we do with our own families.

Ray: It's home, certainly not like a hotel. I'd call our life a community, a household. Whether or not we stay here, whether this house lasts for many years, however, is going to vary from person to person. Probably most of us who are single will marry someday, and whether we stay in a community situation depends on a lot of factors. Maybe the person I marry wouldn't be comfortable with this.

Mary: I know Dan and I will always try to stay with some type of community—if not in the same house, then in another support situation, where your purpose is to help each other out—not only for economic reasons, but to share beliefs as well.

Ray: I can certainly envision what Mary is talking about for married couples: Our lawyer, for example, just bought six row houses with five other couples. Each family lives in a condominium, separately. But they're fixing up a common rec room, and a common kitchen where they'll eat four or five meals a week.

Mary: And each woman won't have to cook every night, they can help each other with the children, taking turns, since they're all married people.

Ray: I think that kind of situation would help things most of the time for married couples. Living here as we do wouldn't be particularly conducive for having children.

Our household worked out better than we anticipated. We've had to struggle at times, to resolve differences of opinion in a trusting manner; but by and large, at least to me, it's surprising how few difficulties there have been. I came from a family of twelve; I'm used to group situations. I've been in some that aren't so good. This one is the most enjoyable and rewarding.

But most people starting out have to be old enough to really share responsibility and to know what they want, what's important, and how they're going to share responsibility. We've got more structure here in dividing the work than you'd need in a smaller group. And we have monthly meetings regularly to work it out, talk about things that might arise.

Mary: We know a lot of shared households, but each one just develops its own style. What we've got took two years to achieve. We worked at it, and we're also getting used to change.

Jerry: Don't focus too much on problems of getting along. I don't see working out relationships as a big thing in this house. We get along.

Georgia: We're getting used to change, as Mary said, in communication, for example. I had a real problem, when I first moved in, in communicating. I think our communications with each other are getting a lot better. I found I need this—to let people know what's going on in me, so they don't start misinterpreting why I'm doing what I'm doing. That was one of the major changes I've seen in myself. I'm sure there are other areas where we've had to change as well.

Ray: Another major change is we started off with three owners, and now everyone is an owner of the house. It's had a good effect: this belongs to all of us. We also are sharing more. Jerry and I are buying a car together, and Jerry and Dan bought a truck together before. I wouldn't have considered anything like that a year ago. Now, I like the idea.

Mary: As for beliefs, most of us are Catholics. That's part of the reason why many of us live in this situation—religious beliefs. It affects our values about lifestyle and the work we want to do.

Ray: And economic reasons—I'm taking a six month leave of absence from my job. I could never afford that if I lived alone.

Dan: We're chartering a yacht for a sailing trip—we couldn't do that if we lived alone. We can also work for ourselves—we have the time and energy to spend time fixing this house together. We couldn't do that if we lived alone and couldn't share our skills. We consider ourselves pretty wealthy.

The Sojourners Community

(Barbara Tamialis, thirty, decided to come to Washington with the Sojourners Community from Chicago in 1975. Married with two small children, she and her husband made this decision in Chicago, after she had completed her master's degree in family studies, because, "we didn't want to live in the nuclear family and do it alone. We needed others who shared our beliefs to help us sustain ourselves as a family. This community was the answer.")

Tamialis is convinced that the nuclear family faces great stress in today's society. Husband and wife, living in isolation, cannot respond in ways to maintain their lives as she and her husband wanted to, she explained. "In this community, the Body of Christ joins us together. As Christians we support each other and don't place the whole burden on the family itself. Parents are responsible to their children. But as Christians, we're also to be sources of ferment in society, support groups for other families. Our community developed so all of us could do this."

Sojourners is an ecumenical community which grew out of an evangelical tradition. "The denominations of members range from nothing to mainly Methodists, Southern Baptists, Mennonites, Plymouth Brethren. Several were raised Catholic," Tamialis explained as she took time out from her supervisory work in the community's daycare center for residents of the lower-income neighborhood.

"Our core-group now numbers sixty. It's a community to which we make a mutual commitment. It's almost hard to become a member. We evolved a novice process, after finding we had to be more careful in accepting members.

"We include families, children, couples, and single persons. Some work in professions in Washington, others work on our magazine, or in our ministries in the neighborhood—the daycare center, tenant organizing, the food club. Others are home with their children. But each of us gives our wages to the community and receives what we need. Monthly costs average $225 per person. Every living unit has a budget.

"We live in four large households with a few people in single apartments or small houses who needed time by themselves. Adults range in age from twenty-five to fifty-two. Every household has its own leadership responsible for relationships in the house. A board of six elders governs the community—they're preoccupied with the vision, the purpose of the community, and part of this is recognizing certain people as household leaders.

"Most of us are here to stay. Everyone in the core is here until they and the community decide they should be elsewhere. What binds us together is essentially our desire to live as New Testament Christians in the world today, searching to know what that means in our families, in our shared lives, and in the witness we give in the world around us.

"Directly in words through our national magazine, in the neighborhood work we do, and in our daily lifestyle, we protest the arms race, the nuclear quest, the destruction of our resources, the lack of love and justice in the world.

"There are others like us. Currently we keep in touch with seven or eight communities across the country that live as formal, committed Christian communities. We're associated with these groups, keep in contact with them.

"We've worked a long time to develop what we have. It came out of much prayer, searching, and reflection, beginning in 1969 when several seminarians in Chicago found themselves in conflict with our country's participation in the Vietnam War. Out of their dialogue grew a magazine, the *Post American,* focusing on pacifism. Some of them lived together, as they worked to resolve their values and needs.

"In September 1975, fifteen of us moved here and began the Sojourners Community as a family. Being here was better for our magazine, and we initially wanted to be near the Church of Our Savior."

In a 1977 issue of *Sojourners,* one of the founders, Jim Wallis, discussed the vision of the community as a community of celebration, celebrating a shared life given by members to help build a more Christian society—beginning first with their own relationships and then expanding outward.

"Building Christ's Body is the foundation of our Community—first in our lives. At the center of this is our worship," he explained.

"We began simply with our own relationship to Jesus Christ, grew to see the implications for our relationships with one another, and now feel a growing connection to a widening circle of people and communities in this country and many places around the world."

Another community member, Jackie Sabath, wrote in the same issue that the search to identify Christian love for one another is the beginning of any ministry or witness we can have. But only when we threw away our own personal agendas, "ceased *reflecting about community* and started thinking about one another" did we begin to have the seeds of building a real community. Before that was strife, struggle, disunity.

Shared life, continued Jim Wallis, came as "we began to think about the simplest kinds of things involved in what it would mean to begin to forgive one another, and to love one another" after initial conflicts in the early struggle for community in Chicago. "We were broken enough that Christ could work among us . . . It took a complete disintegration of our life for us to begin to learn some of those lessons"—of honesty, dependence on God, and love for each other.

Sabath described the pastoral leadership which lay at the heart of the community. A leadership that has to do with more than decision-making, "It has most to do with pastoring . . . nurturing . . . disciplining . . . teaching." One which serves all.

This witness, the community believes, must also be political. As Wallis concluded in a *Sojourners* editorial recently, their commitment is twofold: to study the times and to support a growing community of persons "who are allowing the gospel to radically change their personal and corporate lives" and to work politically as "loving adversaries of the status quo and joyful creators of new possibilities . . . "

The Bible, Wallis said, shows God sides with the poor, brings a new system of sharing, simplicity, division of goods, helping the poor. Now is a time when the state and the structures of economic power "have created the imminent danger of nuclear holocaust."

To live the Christian life in this challenge, he concluded, we need one another.

FOR REVIEW AND REFLECTION

Write a reaction to each of the three communities interviewed in this chapter, using the questions on page 169.

Relationships 14
in the World Family

Our Future and Our Values

Do you think about the future very often? Have headlines and TV shows about gas and housing prices made you wonder what your own future will be like? Or what kind of life you will live with your own family someday?

We took a brief poll not long ago, asking four persons about their feelings toward the future. "How do you feel about it? What comes to your mind when you think about the future?" we asked.

"I'm gonna have a hard time," responded Tim. "I won't be able to have money as I'll need it," he said.

Sarah said, "In my future there'll be wild prices. If everything goes as bad as it seems, it'll be like the Depression."

Chuck focused on new ways to live. "We'll have solar energy and underground housing. I expect hard times in my future."

Penny thought about relationships. "It'll be back to the basics. We'll be a lot less mobile. Neighborhoods will come to mean more. Life will be better, fun; families will mean more."

Each of the four saw something different in the future. What would your answer have been?

Our reactions to the future vary. The future can be many things—harder for some of us, easier for others—depending on what we value.

Recently some national leaders have begun to predict that the future will force us to lower our living standards. Most of them—and most of us—equate this with a "worse" life. Less growth in the Gross National Product, we are told, means a worse life. But are the two the same? Does economic gain necessarily mean human growth or quality of life or happiness? Growing industries which pollute the air and make people sick incur costs we have not really begun to measure. Living in a lovely home and driving two cars does not guarantee a happy life or good family relationships. Much more is involved in human growth, in what makes a "worse" or "better" life.

Whether you are apprehensive or hopeful about the future, one thing is certain: the future promises rapid change, as we discussed much earlier in this course. Change will have a profound impact on our personal lives, our friendships, and our love relationships.

How will your relationships be affected? Will happy times be fewer, love more fragile? Take your own poll. Ask others what they think.

No matter what we expect, our feelings about lifestyle have effects on our relationships. If we believe that happiness comes from living in a certain kind of home, wearing certain kinds of clothes, being able to eat and recreate in certain ways, driving certain kinds of cars where and when we want, relationships very likely will suffer. Challenging choices are required. Relationships require time and energy—an investment of ourselves. A world of shrinking resources makes us face our needs and values. As individuals, and as a nation, will it be goods and rewards or persons we value most?

As North Americans, members of the richest technological society on earth, our decisions about growth can mean life or death for millions of people. For, literally, we have been consuming the world. In this course we have discussed relationships in our private lives. If we continue to pursue consumer relationships with the earth and the rest of the human family, however, there will be no growth or peace for the user or the used.

The World Is Like a Living Cell

In an era of connections, our choices in regard to personal, environmental, and international relationships merge to become moral questions. The biologist Lewis Thomas wrote in **The Lives of a Cell** that the earth and all that is in it are connected in ways "most like a single cell."

In the past it was easy to ignore this, he continued. The earth, we thought, "was man's personal property, a combination of garden, zoo, bank vault, and energy source, placed at our disposal to be consumed, ornamented, or pulled apart as we wished . . . Mastery over nature, mystery and all, was a moral duty and social obligation."

But we have learned a lot, he reminded us. Everything is not clear yet, but most agree "that we are not the masters of nature that we thought . . . we are as dependent on the rest of life as are the leaves or midges or fish. Humans are part of the system"—the world cell.

Yet humans try to dominate the environment and each other. Thomas would prefer another role, one demanding we change in our basic attitudes toward each other. We should see the world family itself as a "natural resource," to be worried over. If we were more aware of what is most wonderful in humanity, we might try to protect ourselves "as a valuable, endangered species. We couldn't lose."

Thomas is talking about an era of connections when it is no longer possible to ignore the relationship between an ocean oil spill and the price of fish in the store, between abundant beef and hungry people in poorer nations. It is an era in which Christ's words—that we are one in him—take on more real meaning.

Members of the world family are closely linked. Today's headlines remind us of this fact continuously:

RICH NATIONS' WANTS VS. POOR NATIONS' NEEDS

HUNGER STALKS THE EARTH

WORLD RUNNING OUT OF FUEL

Or we hear phrases like "polluted oceans," "greenhouse effect," or "acid rain."

Our consumer society, based on technology, is only beginning to recognize the earth's limits, human needs, and human connectedness.

Many people are beginning to ask, "Is there another way to grow, one that values people over profit?"

Living and working in a technological society separates people, organizations, even countries, from one another. Yet as world resources shrink and human needs expand, people have become more **interdependent.**

In October 1979, Pope John Paul II brought this message to the United States. In a speech to 80,000 persons gathered for Mass in Yankee Stadium, he reminded us of our connections to the rest of the world. "We cannot stand idly by enjoying our own riches and freedom if in any place the Lazarus of the twentieth century stands at our doors," he said.

Live in simpler ways, he urged the thousands: "decisively break with a frenzy of consumerism, [which is] exhausting and joyless." "It is not right that the standard of living of the rich countries should seek to maintain itself by draining off a great part of the reserves of energy and raw materials that are meant to serve the whole human family."

He told us that America in particular can no longer escape the effects of its lifestyle on the rest of mankind. We are called to respond in personal and public ways to end the suffering and danger we bring to the world's men, women, and children.

What is the relationship he described? Do we know, for example, that as Americans, comprising 6 percent of the world's population, we consume one-third of the world's petroleum, more than half the natural gas, and one-third of most of the energy resources? Do we know that, by the year 2000, our world of 4 billion men, women, and children will increase to more than 6 billion? That half of our world's population lives in the 90 to 95 countries where hunger is rampant? That most of the population growth (90 percent) will occur in those poorer nations? That by the year 2000, Mexico, for example, will grow almost 20 percent—to become half the size of the United States?

Do we know that in this growing world family we live as a rich and defensive hoarder, consuming a major share of the world's energy and goods while arming to guard ourselves and others against the disorder we help create?

The opening pages of **Taking Charge,** written by John Shippee, describe the world family this way: "If the world were a global village of 100 people, 6 of them would be Americans. These 6 would have over a third of the village's income and the other 94 would subsist on the other two-thirds. How would the wealthy 6 live 'in peace' with their neighbors?" It is a village, we read, where 47 cannot read, 1 is college-educated, 35 are hungry and malnourished, and half or more lack homes or adequate housing. To get the resources we consume, we belong to a select group of rich nations who get over 81 percent of their raw materials from the poorest nations.

Our system programs the world's poor into continued inferiority in their trade and development programs. Poor nations, who gear their agriculture and production to our needs at our prices, must import food, goods, and energy at inflated world prices. Third world nations who once fed themselves now hunger because their agricultural development goes into "cash" crops for export.

In this world village where many children in poor nations face severe malnutrition, $160 is spent yearly on each child, and $16,000 on each soldier. There are "more explosives than food" in this village, a world military expert says. The United States is the world's largest producer of these arms.

Do we know our food choices in this village require land, food, and energy beyond all proportion to our own size? It takes 21 pounds of plant protein to produce 1 pound of beef protein, wasting 18,000,000 tons of grain annually.

Our national diet is centered on beef and uses up most of our grain harvest as well as imports from poor nations. Seventeen times more land is required for a person on a milk-and-meat-centered diet than for a person on a plant protein diet. We feed more grain to livestock than is consumed in all of India and China—one-third of the world. Thirty percent of the world's population, in the rich nations, consume half the world's food. Yet if the food supply were evenly divided, says Robert Simon in **Bread for the World,** it would feed us all.

Jesus on Wealth

Being wealthy is not compatible with real charity, Jesus told us over and over. Christ's strongest teaching, his call to love and share with the poor, demands that we recognize our relationships to others in the world family. It is on this that we will be judged, he said clearly in Matthew 25:31-37:

> **When the Son of Man comes in his glory and all the angels with him, he will sit in state on his throne, with all the nations gathered before him. He will separate men into two groups, as a shepherd separates the sheep from the goats, and he will place the sheep on his right hand, the goats on his left. Then the king will say to those on his right hand, "You have my Father's blessing; come, enter and possess the kingdom that has been ready for you since the world was made. For when I was hungry, you gave me food; when thirsty, you gave me drink; when I was a stranger, you took me into your home; when naked you clothed me; when I was ill you came to my help; when in prison you visited me."**

So strong was his emphasis on detachment from possessions, that we have to conclude that real Christians do not accumulate wealth. Jesus condemned the hollow gifts of the rich and praised the widow's mite (Luke 21:1-4). "Don't store up for yourselves treasures on earth," he reminded us in Matthew 6:19-21, "for where your treasure is, there will your heart be also."

John Paul II, in calling Americans to bridge the gap between rich and poor in the world, merely repeated Christ's mandate to love. It demands the action John spoke about in his first letter recalling the fundamentals of faith: "But if a man has enough to live on and yet when he sees his brother in need shuts up his heart against him, how can it be said that the divine love dwells in him? My child, love must not be a matter of words or talk; it must be genuine, and show itself in action."

The gap John Paul II condemned reflects our choices as individuals and as a nation. But in a country where, Robert Simon reminds us, the "ordinary person can help shape those policies," the most urgent way we can respond to world hunger is to "contact leaders in government on issues that vitally affect hungry people." For we cannot avoid responsibility for our relationships to the world family.

Living Simply

The era of "no limits" is at an end. The pleas of hungry children in Africa, landless peasants in South America, and the poor even in our own nation feed the disorder we rally to arm ourselves against. The needs of our world family, stated John Paul II, face us in the most intimate relationships, in the privacy of our homes and apartments. It is a time to live simply, he reminds us, in lives that reflect our connections to humankind, and to Christ. For the first time in the history of the world, even our survival depends on the acceptance of Jesus and his lifestyle message for us.

John Shippee in **Taking Charge** describes how the process of simple living affects relations on several levels. As we look for creative ways to find our own economic alternatives, lessening our dependencies on the corporations which dominate the world's economic relationships, we find ourselves changing, growing, feeling satisfaction in our own families and friendships.

As we seek to live more simply, we are forced to ask ourselves what it is that makes life good—physically, psychologically, and spiritually. A person who begins with questions about what to buy, eat, wear, what energy to use, soon grows to ask what brings happiness in family events, friendship, marriage, in the work he or she does. It also means trying to create fun with people on holidays and on special occasions instead of trying to buy it. What do you enjoy about Christmas most?

Can you think of ways that simplicity at Christmas would help you enjoy family more than things? sharing time more than sharing products?

Simplicity means searching for ways to make family time richer, to help persons enjoy each other more.

Simple living means evenings at the dinner table when family members ask, "What do we really need? How can we share more? What would really make this house happy? this meal joyful? this evening fun?"

If our jobs leave us little time for one another, for our spouse, friends, or children, simplicity helps us to ask, "Does what we earn bring us closer or merely buy us things we don't really need?"

Simplicity forces us to be creative instead of merely acquiring. It offers us a basis for lasting friendships, stripping away fake needs in favor of real ones.

A Case Study

For some, simplicity makes the important things in life possible by freeing up time and money for better uses. John and Joan Richards, a married couple in their late thirties, with two children, made a drastic lifestyle change a few years ago so that they could work and live in ways

that were important to them. It meant rejecting a good paying, prestigious, and secure job. It also meant they had a relationship which could allow them to do this.

Read the following description of how their decision not only affected but grew out of the relationship they share. As you read, ask yourself how their marriage would have been different if they had kept a lifestyle which ran counter to their values and their needs for real growth.

What does a decision like this demand of a married couple on a day-to-day basis? What can they gain from such an attempt to do what they believe? What do they risk?

John tells his view of their life in the last six years:

I was vice-president of a bank and had spent nine years working my way up to my position. But I finally realized I didn't like being in banking and all the administrative and political sorts of things I had to do. I also wanted to do something professionally on my own. This, coupled with war protests, made me realize I didn't belong in the banking business.

It was scary, but I quit my job and took a job with a friend. It didn't work out and we lost a lot of money. At this point, a change in lifestyle developed for my wife and me, and we soon came to the point where both of us were working at whatever we could just to make ends meet. We were thirty-one and had been married two years.

I'm a sculptor now by profession, but I can't make a living on what I make as an artist—maybe someday I will—so I work at carpentry to help maintain our family. There have been times when I have been able to do sculpturing most of the year, but for the last two years I haven't been able to do as much.

Economically, we went through a period where we didn't know where next month's income would come from. It affected us economically in a lot of ways, made us very conscious of what we wanted to do with our money if there were any available. Finally now, because of the carpentry business, we have an income that's a little more secure . . .

Joan is more qualified than I at a lot of things in our home—in handling a lot of the parenting, nurturing of the children, for example. But our lifestyle has made us deal with sharing this more than we would have otherwise. I do more than most fathers, I think, but she's better at it. Our lifestyle change involved working out a flexible system of housekeeping and those sorts of things. We share a lot—there's certain things she doesn't like to do that I do. I do the dishes, and we have family cleanup sessions to take care of housekeeping, that sort of thing.

Consciousness about world conditions has really brought us to try to live simply, as well. So we took a year off. I built a solar energy system on a building because I think it's important not to leave this to the politicians.

I got a grant for my solar unit from the state, but my lifestyle also gave us the opportunity to do that, to be able to say, "Well, I know that it's going to make things kind of goofy for a while, but if I, if we, really work it through and try these ideas, then I think we're better people for it."

It's a sacrifice for both of us. I mean, I like to do it, I get a real bang out of it, and Joan has been willing to let me have that time.

I think she's shared my values pretty much. We sort of grew together. We were originally a couple of middle-class kids who got married and fell out of bed together in the sixties. All of this has changed our relationship too: there's more freedom. It's hard to pin down, to remember what we used to be, but it's changed our relationship, living like this.

The thing that made going through all these changes possible, and also made it bearable whenever there was any difficulty, was the ability to sit down and say what I'm thinking. But that's what communication is, and when we do that, we really work closely together, and it's just a super relationship.

It always is, but it has ups and downs; when we both get busy—we both have jobs—life goes at a pretty hectic pace. She's been able to pursue things she's interested in too. She has a new job she's excited about. The one thing that I sometimes worry about is that I've had all the freedom and she's had a lot of sacrifices; as long as she's content with it, I'm OK. If she ever got out of phase with things, I think I'd have to get a regular job.

Would I do it? Sure. I wouldn't like it too much, but I would. You see, our marriage is too good a relationship to mess with.

John was interviewed at work, in an old house he was remodeling.

Joan, in a letter to the author, wrote these comments about how their lifestyle affected their marriage, and vice versa:

> I think the most important aspect of any marriage relationship—with children or without them—is communication. If two people can talk honestly about their needs and pleasures, their feelings, then many other problems can be avoided.
>
> One of the things I think it is important to talk regularly about is the "division of labor"—without cultural biases. Who is working outside the home? Who is going to care for the children? Or how are we going to divide that? What jobs need to be done in the home? Who likes to do which of these? Is anyone feeling burdened? Are everyone's needs being met by this particular arrangement—children's? parents'?
>
> We have had some trouble overcoming our own cultural biases, but with our children it isn't that way. Our boys don't have those built-in expectations. Maybe someday we'll overcome that dreadful custom of the women retiring to the kitchen after dinner and the men to the living room. There's hope!

What feelings do you get about their marriage? Is it strong? Have they grown in closeness? trust? generosity? Have they grown as individuals as well? Has growth been a shared process for them?

Notice what each describes as important: simple, normal events of daily life, the conversation at the table at the end of the day, asking honestly how to approach work, spend money, or share parenting.

As Joan and John grew as individuals their friendship also deepened. As a process, it came through daily efforts to communicate, to care, to be supportive, to ask: "What do you need? What do I need?" "How are we feeling about this?" "Are we being honest?" "What is most important to us all in this choice?" "What do we share that makes us happy?" "Should we buy this?"

Many persons fear the eighties. They think the end of a lifestyle of affluence means the end of good living. But in an era when our connections with the world family and with the earth come together, we can build new and richer relationships with friends, with nations, with the earth itself. Christ's message was clear: life becomes simple when it is well lived. Living well means loving well. And our own lives depend on it.

The Shakertown Pledge

In 1974 at the Yokefellow Institute in Richmond, Indiana, a group of religious retreat center directors and their staffs gathered with others—as a followup to a meeting at Shakertown, Kentucky—to make a common pledge of responsibility to the world's problems by which they could live and commend to others. Called the Shakertown Pledge in honor of the original gathering place and the Shakers who had believed in lives of "creative simplicity," the following is the pledge:

Recognizing that the earth and the fullness thereof is a gift from our gracious God, and that we are called to cherish, nurture, and provide loving stewardship for the earth's resources, and recognizing that life itself is a gift, and a call to responsibility, joy, and celebration,

I make the following declarations:

1. I declare myself to be a world citizen.
2. I commit myself to lead an ecologically sound life.
3. I commit myself to lead a life of creative simplicity and to share my personal wealth with the world's poor.
4. I commit myself to join with others in the reshaping of institutions in order to bring about a more just global society in which all people have full access to the needed resources for their physical, emotional, intellectual, and spiritual growth.
5. I commit myself to occupational accountability, and so doing I will seek to avoid the creation of products which cause harm to others.
6. I affirm the gift of my body and commit myself to its proper nourishment and physical well-being.
7. I commit myself to examine continually my relationships with others, and to attempt to relate honestly, morally, and lovingly to those around me.
8. I commit myself to personal renewal through prayer, meditation, and study.
9. I commit myself to responsible participation in a community of faith.

FOR REVIEW AND REFLECTION

1) Looking at the four responses to the question "What comes to your mind when you think about the future?" (page 177), which response seems correct in your mind? What response would you give? Explain briefly.

2) Which of the following items are the most important Christian concerns, in your mind? Rearrange these items into a new list, ranking them in their order of importance:

hunger in the world	abortion
sexism	sexual permissiveness
racism	pollution
war	birth control
energy shortages	maintaining our high
saving wildlife	standard of living

Explain in some detail: What did you list first? Why?

3) At this point in your life, could you sign the Shakertown Pledge? Why? Why not?

Acknowledgments continued from page 4.

professional fields, states of life, and lifestyles, who at different stages in the research agreed to be interviewed and so generously shared their ideas and experiences with me; and most of all to my husband and children, for their continued patience and support, and to Steve Nagel, for his determined but kindly prodding and thoughtful guidance. I hope this book meets some of their expectations for a text on a subject so important today, yet so devoid of clear or certain answers.

Grateful acknowledgment is made for permission to print: Selections from *Culture and Commitment* by Margaret Mead, copyright 1970, 1978 by Margaret Mead. Reprinted by permission of Doubleday and Company, Inc. Cartoon from *The Ziggy Treasury* by Tom Wilson, copyright 1977, Universal Press Syndicate, Inc. Reprinted by permission of Andrews and McMeel, Inc. Cartoon from *The Cathy Chronicles* by Cathy Guisewite, copyright 1978 by Universal Press Syndicate, Inc. Reprinted by permission of Andrews and McMeel, Inc. Poem titled "Warning" from *Once*, copyright 1968 by Alice Walker. Reprinted by permission of Harcourt Brace Jovanovich, Inc. Poem titled "For Every Woman" by Nancy R. Smith. Reprinted by permission of The Upper Room.

Illustrations: John Arms, pages 20, 107, 137; Rohn Engh, pages 74, 80, 120, 140, 146, 185; Jack Hamilton, pages 12, 43, 109; Jean-Claude LeJeune, page 158; Steve Murray, page 65; NC Photos, page 132; Norman Provost, FSC, pages 2, 23, 28, 33, 40, 79, 116, 164, 178; Ron Sievert, page 35; Dalia Sudavicius, page 127; Taurus Photos, pages 8, 52, 61, 104, 119; Wallowitch, pages 143, 150, 153; Phillip MacMillan James, cover.